Techniques of Translation:
Chaucer's *Boece*

by
Tim William Machan

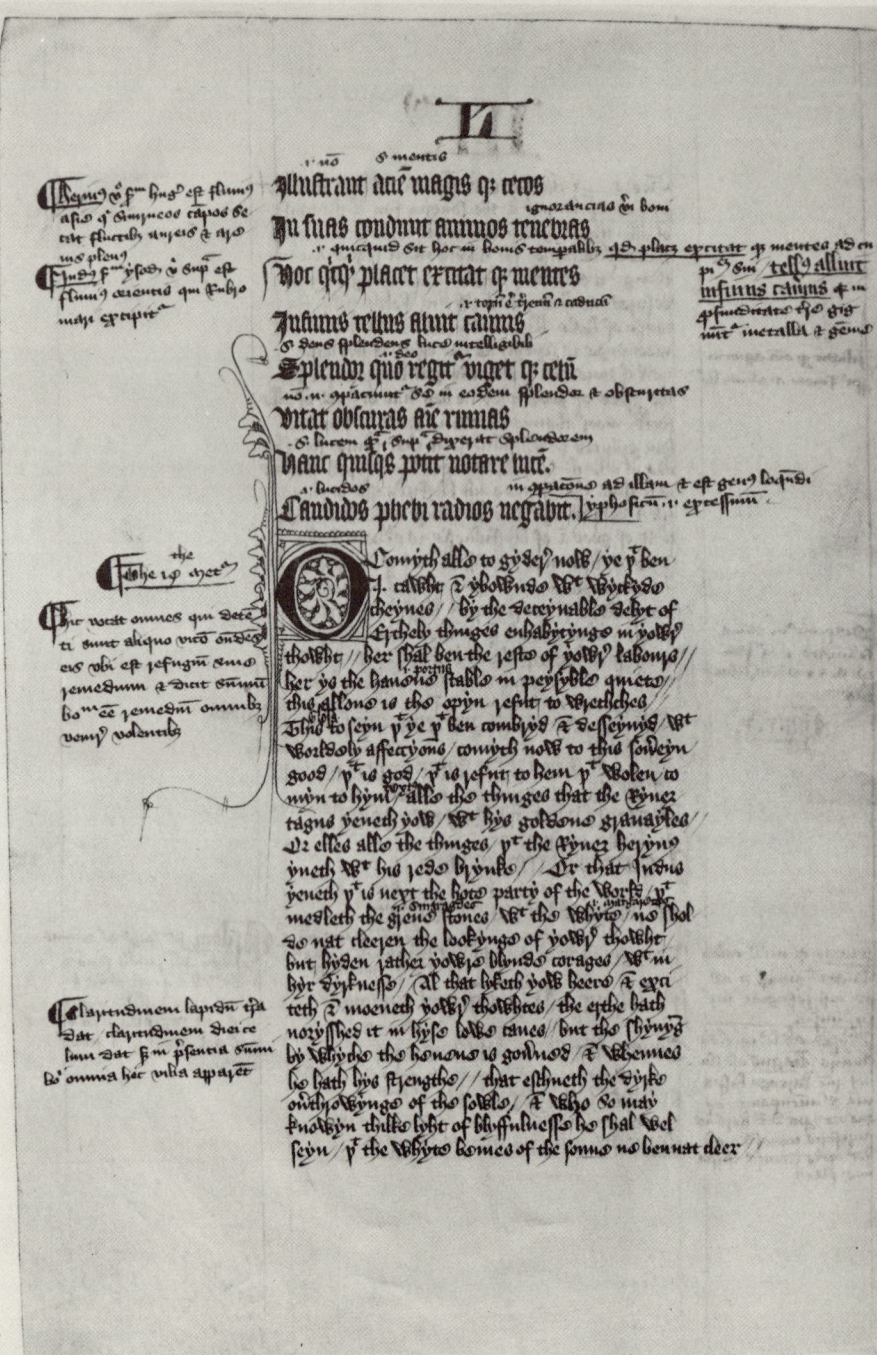

A leaf from MS Cambridge Ii. 3. 21, reprinted by permission of the Syndics of Cambridge University Library.

TECHNIQUES OF TRANSLATION:
CHAUCER'S *BOECE*

by TIM WILLIAM MACHAN

PILGRIM BOOKS
NORMAN, OKLAHOMA

Library of Congress Cataloging in Publication Data
Machan, Tim William.
    Techniques of translation.

    Bibliography: p.
    Includes index.
    1. Chaucer, Geoffrey, d. 1400 — Technique.
2. Boethius, d. 524 — Translations, English.
3. Boethius, d. 524. De consolatione philosophiae.
4. Latin language — Translating into English.
5. French language — To 1500 — Translating into English. I. Title.
PR1940.M29   1985   821'.1   85-524
ISBN 0-937664-68-5

Copyright ©1985 by Pilgrim Books, Inc., Norman, Oklahoma, Manufactured in the U.S.A. First edition.

For Christine

Contents

	Foreword and Acknowledgments	ix
1	Medieval Translation, Chaucer and *Boece*	1
2	Words	11
3	Syntax	59
4	Style	85
5	The Implications of Chaucer's Technique	111
6	Towards an Evaluation of Chaucer as Translator	125
	Notes	133
	Bibliography	149
	Index of Lines	157
	Index of Names and Terms	161

FOREWORD

For all the initial analyses for this book, I used typescript copies of the Latin, French and English texts prepared by Jerome Taylor and myself for the *Variorum Boece*. Since a publication date has not yet been established for that book, however, and since the line numbers of the typescripts will not coincide with those of the printed edition, I have converted all citations to the Latin text of Bieler (1957), the French text of Dedeck-Héry (1952) and the English text of Robinson (1957). When these texts differ significantly from those of the *Variorum*, I have emended them accordingly and have cited the difference in a footnote (see further p. 7 and note 17). In the second chapter, for the sake of clarity, I have also occasionally omitted Latin and French enclitics. Unless otherwise indicated, punctuation is as it appears in the various editions, with the following exceptions: I have omitted the italicization of Robinson and Dedeck-Héry and have supplied, when necessary, Bieler's text with quotation marks. All quotations of Chaucer's other works are also from Robinson's edition.

ACKNOWLEDGMENTS

I should first like to express my debt and gratitude to Jerome Taylor, under whose direction an early version of this study was written; his critical acumen, exacting standards and fairness are the best of inspirations. I am also grateful to Paul G. Ruggiers, who saw promise in this study and offered many perceptive criticisms. Others who have helped in a variety of important ways are: Douglas Kelly, Fannie Lemoine, Dan Ransom, Donald W. Rowe and Charles T. Scott. I should also like to thank the Graduate School at the University of Wisconsin-Madison for its financial support. My greatest debt is expressed in the dedication. I alone, of course, am responsible for all of the opinions and conclusions offered herein.

TWM
Madison, Wisconsin
November, 1984

Techniques of Translation:
Chaucer's *Boece*

by
Tim William Machan

CHAPTER 1

MEDIEVAL TRANSLATION, CHAUCER AND *BOECE*

One may suspect that Chaucer, surveying from the *Galaxye* our literary and philological antics upon the *litel erthe that heer is . . . so ful of torment and of hard grace*, would prefer the Philological Society to the Royal Society of Literature, and an editor of the English Dictionary to a poet laureate. Not that Chaucer *redivivus* would be a phonologist or a lexicographer rather than a popular writer — *the lyf so short, the craft so long to lerne!* But certainly, as far as treatment of himself goes (and he had a well-formed opinion of the value of his own work), of all the words and ink posterity has spent or spilt over his entertaining writings, he would chiefly esteem the efforts to recover the detail of what he wrote, even (indeed particularly) down to the forms and spellings, to recapture an idea of what it sounded like, to make certain what it meant. Let the source-hunter *have his swink to him reserved*. For Chaucer was interested in "language," and in the forms of his own tongue. (Tolkien, 1934:1)

When attempting to interpret and evaluate Chaucer, as when interpreting and evaluating any writer, a number of topics need to be considered: life, canon, metrics, poetics, narrative techniques, characterization, and literary debts and influences. All of these are aspects of Chaucer the writer, and all of them contribute to our understanding of Chaucer's achievement. Yet Chaucer, unlike many other authors, was also a translator, and this aspect of his work has scarcely been discussed. By translator here I do not mean adaptor, for there are numerous insightful studies of how Chaucer altered the narratives, themes and images of Boccaccio, for instance, to his own designs.[1] Adaptations such as the *Troilus* or the *Book of the Duchess* may be considered varieties of translation, and indeed it is likely that Deschamps labeled Chaucer "le grant translateur" for just this type of work. But Chaucer has so thoroughly taken possession of *Il Filostrato*, for example, that one does not, indeed cannot, speak of the mechanics of how he rendered Boccaccio's Italian syntax and lexicon into English.

For by translation I intend reproduction. There is a good deal of latitude, of course, in the form such reproduction can take. On the one hand, a translation may imitate the lexicon and syntax of its source; on the other, it may simply attempt to capture the sense; or it may even take a middle way, capturing the sense by only partially naturalizing the grammar.[2] But whether one classifies translations in a bipartite or tripartite system, it is clear that a translation, but not an adaptation, attempts to reproduce the meaning of the source and not to utilize the source in the production of an original composition.

Although all of this is well-known, there are still problems involved in discussing Chaucer the translator, and these problems perhaps account for the critical neglect of this aspect of his writing. For instance, it is not at all clear what Chaucer himself understood by translation, for he uses the term to describe both the *Romaunt* and the *Troilus* (see below p. 5). While modern scholars would agree with the classification of the former work, the latter, as has just been noted, is best regarded as an adaptation. Most critics would also say that *Boece*, the *Melibee* and the *Parson's Tale* are translations, while the *Knight's Tale* is an adaptation. Yet, given current understanding of Chaucer's translation techniques and of how he himself understood translation, there is still uncertainty as to which of the Chaucerian works is in fact a translation. Thus, it has recently been suggested by Lipson (1983) that the *Astrolabe*, traditionally regarded as a translation, is best considered an example of Chaucer's own prose. In any event, it is recognized that translations constitute a large part of the Chaucerian canon,[3] and though the sources and artistic merits of most of what are generally considered translations have been discussed, the actual mechanics of Chaucer's translation technique remain relatively unexplored.[4]

Given the importance attached to translation in the Middle Ages, however, the critical neglect of Chaucer's translation technique is indeed unfortunate. For instance, Chaucer thought highly of translation, as is indicated by the number of translations he wrote. Moreover, translation was an especially prolific source of literature in medieval England, and Richard Green (1980) has shown how much translations and devotional pieces figured in the advancement of a medieval author. It should be remembered that in the *Retraction* to the *Canterbury Tales*, *Boece*, a translation, is the only work Chaucer cites by name of those for which he gives thanks to "oure Lord Jhesu Crist and his blisful Mooder, and alle the seintes of hevene" (*CT*.X.1089). Furthermore, despite the number of translations composed in medieval England, understanding of the theory and practice of medieval translation in general, compared to understanding of medieval poetics, is still regrettably inadequate.[5] To be sure, there have been advances in the area. Sven Fristedt (1953, 1969, 1973) has itemized the Wycliffite's techniques, Traugott Lawler (1983) has examined Trevisa's, and Roger Ellis (1982) has identified the choices made by medieval translators in general. It is now clear, for instance, that the translators of the second Wycliffite Bible "opened up" (for which see Chapter Three) more closed Latin constructions than did those of the first, and that Trevisa in his translation of Bartholomaeus's *De Proprietatibus Rerum* emphasized accuracy over clarity, the reverse of his procedure in his earlier translation of Higden's *Polychronicon*. It is also clear that the range of choices a medieval translator had to make—including source, form, lexicon, grammar and style—was as wide as that faced by a modern counterpart. But translators treated their sources in a wide variety of ways, and many aspects of medieval translation remain unexplored. For instance, we do not know, in many cases, why a translator made the choices he did, who the audience of his translation was, and what the objectives of his translation were. Without answers to such questions, we have no standards by which to evaluate a given translation; we cannot know if a translator's techniques combine cohesively or how a given translation compares to others of its sort—since the sorts are ill-defined—or to all translations in general. In short, without understanding of the objectives and techniques in individual medieval translations, such as already exist for Trevisa's and the Wicliffites',[6] the ranking of medieval translations is unwarranted and invalid. Indeed, the diversity of the types of translation in the Middle Ages may preclude the concept of *a* medieval theory of translation. Rigorous analysis is needed, for "flowing syntax" and "Latinate vocabulary" are not critical terms.

Part of the problem in evaluating medieval translations, of course, is that the translators themselves say so little about their techniques and objectives. Trevisa and the author of the so-called Purvey preface to the second Wicliffite Bible,[7] both of whom will be considered in detail in Chapter Three, are eloquent exceptions, but the majority of medieval translators are either silent or very general in describing their techniques. Many translators refer only to St. Jerome's famous dictum "non verbum e verbo, sed sensum exprimere sensu,"[8] but, as Samuel Workman (1940:76) has indicated, this phrase became little more than a convention in the Middle Ages and was applied to any translation, however an author translated his sources.[9] An individual translator may indicate his intended audience, his treatment of difficult words, or the alterations he has made of his original,[10] but no translator provides a detailed examination of all the techniques he uses. Even the explicitness of the Purvey preface is only apparent, for of the many Latin grammatical structures, the author mentions only ablative absolutes, participles, relative pronouns and word order. Of course, it is not surprising that medieval translators generally remain silent about their techniques; in many cases, the translators themselves were probably unaware of the diverse ways in which they responded to their sources. That is, the grammar of translation, like the grammar of spoken language, may be largely internalized. Moreover, what matters to any reading audience is the faithful reproduction of the content of the original, or the readability of the translation, not *how* the translator achieves the reproduction or readability. Furthermore, from a different perspective, medieval linguistics, as practiced by the "modistae," was theoretical rather than purely descriptive.

In this regard, then, it is not remarkable that Chaucer, despite the number of translations he composed, should also be silent about his technique. Indeed, he cannot be said to espouse a theory, for when he does comment on translation, it is from the conventional Hieronymic posture:

> ... in my sentence,
> Shul ye nowher fynden difference
> Fro the sentence of this tretys lyte
> After the which this murye tale I write.
> (*CT*.VII.961-64)[11]

The reference in the prologue to the *Astrolabe* to "full light reules and naked wordes" is Chaucer's most explicit statement on the issue. Moreover, Chaucer, like many of his contemporaries, occasionally did not distinguish between translation and adaptation, as is witnessed by Alceste's comment:

> ... this man is nyce,
> He may translate a thyng in no malyce,
> But for he useth bokes for to make,
> And taketh non hed of what matere he take,
> Therfore he wrot the Rose and ek Crisseyde
> Of innocence, and nyste what he seyde.
> (*LGW*g.340-45)[12]

Chaucer's silence about his translation technique, however, should not be echoed by a critical silence, for, as was mentioned above, translations constitute a large part of the Chaucerian canon; if we are to make a fair evaluation of Chaucer the writer, we need to consider Chaucer the translator. The inadequacy of current knowledge and the diversity of Chaucer's translations prevent categorical statements. His technique was undoubtedly tailored to his objectives for, and the demands of, individual works; in the *Clerk's Tale* and the *Melibee* Chaucer had to accommodate his sources to specific pilgrims in the *Canterbury Tales* framework, in the *Astrolabe* (and possibly the *Equatorie of the Planetis*) he was faced with a technical source, and in the *Parson's Tale*, *Boece* and the lost translation of Pope Innocent's *De Contemptu Mundi* with theological and philosophical ones. But it is also clear that there is something Chaucerian in all the translations, so that Chaucer's use of certain techniques will eventually allow us to evaluate his relationship to other medieval translators. The knowledge to make such an evaluation, however, can be acquired only through understanding of Chaucer's techniques in individual translations. Caroline Eckhardt (1984) has already examined the *Romaunt*; the present study explores *Boece*.

The influence of the *Consolation of Philosophy* on Chaucer is well-known; the ideas of the *Consolation* inform, among other works, the *Knight's Tale*, the *Wife of Bath's Tale*, the *Troilus* and the so-called Boethian balades. Although only two of the nine extant manuscripts attribute *Boece* to Chaucer,[13] Chaucer refers to the work on three occasions (*LGW*f.425, *CT*.X.1088 and *Adam*.2) and his authorship is not in doubt. Chaucer may have composed the translation on Jean de Meung's suggestion in the *Roman de la Rose*—

> In Boece of Consolacioun...
> Where lewid men myght lere wit,
> Whoso that wolde translaten it
> (*Rom*.5661, 5665-66)[14]—

but when he did so is uncertain. One might venture a date of 1380, but for *Boece*, as for most of Chaucer's works, hard evidence is lacking.[15] *Boece* evidently circulated during Chaucer's lifetime, for Usk utilized it in his *Testament of Love* (c. 1387), and the artistry of Chaucer's prose was praised by Shirley, Lydgate and (later) Caxton.[16] But Chaucer's translation apparently held little interest for subsequent readers, for Caxton's is the most recent comment on it in Spurgeon's *Five Hundred Years of Chaucer Criticism*. Modern critics have also displayed little interest in *Boece*, despite the fact that numerous studies have been written on the "Boethian element" in Chaucer's poetry.

Many early critics, believing *Boece* to be a translation of Boethius's *De Consolatione Philosophiae* alone, chastized Chaucer for his alleged inadequacies as a Latinist. In H. F. Stewart's famous assessment (1891:226),

> [W]hile no one can deny that the translation abounds with slipshod renderings, with awkward phrases and downright glaring mistakes of a kind to make a modern examiner's hair stand on end, yet its inaccuracy and infelicity is not that of an inexperienced Latin scholar, but rather of one who was no Latin scholar at all.

Similar sentiments are expressed by Liddell (1897 and 1898), Chute (1946:156) and French (1947:122), while D. S. Brewer (1953:64), on the other hand, has maintained that the "translation was written with scholarly care." An approach as pedantic as Stewart's is fruitless for any translation and in the case of *Boece* also misguided, for Chaucer utilized both the *Consolatio* and Jean de Meung's translation of the Latin, *Li Livres de Confort de Philosophie* (see Lowes, 1917 and Dedeck-Héry, 1937), the possibility of which Stewart (1891:204-6) in fact recognized. Indeed, *Boece* is heavily indebted to the French, where many of Chaucer's "mistakes" have their source. Moreover, the Latin text Chaucer used was not identical to the modern editions consulted by scholars. As Kottler (1953) shows, a "vulgate" version of the *Consolatio* existed in the later Middle Ages, and this version is substantively different from that found in the earliest manuscripts of the *Consolatio*, upon which all modern editions are based. It was a Latin manuscript—and the distinction between manuscript and standardized text is important—within the vulgate tradition, as well as a frequently corrupt French manuscript, Nicholas Trevet's commentary and the Remigian glosses on the *Consolatio*, that Chaucer consulted.[17]

Another tendency in *Boece* scholarship has been to regard the translation as an original composition and to assess accordingly its literary merits. Such an approach results in conclusions which are as contradictory as those reached by grading *Boece* as if it were written by a modern scholar. Thus, George Saintsbury (1907:213) contends that *Boece* is "literature within and without" and that in the meters

> we have . . . for the first time in Middle English, distinctly ornate prose, aureate in vocabulary, rhythmical in cadence and setting an example which, considering the popularity both of author and translator, could not fail to be of the greatest importance in the history of our literature.

Similarly, Root (1934:85) sees in *Boece* "a dignity and eloquence that suggest the perfection, three centuries later, of this same tradition of rhetorical prose in the hands of John Milton." On the other hand, George Krapp (1915:10) suggests that Chaucer "wisely made little effort to introduce specifically English ornaments of style," while George Cowling (1927:98) contends that Chaucer uses "a horny English, vivid enough at times, but lacking both texture and rhythmical swing." One of the most common critical responses to *Boece* is to compare it to Chaucer's poetic adaptations of the *Consolation*, always to the detriment of the former; so ten Brink (1870:141), Stewart (1891:227-28), Krapp (1915:10), Patch (1935:69), Anderson (1950:151) and Fisher (1977:815). But, as Ralph Elliott (1974:168) has suggested,

> The point of contrasting passages from *Boece* with corresponding passages in the poems is not to render the former absurd by comparison, but to illustrate Chaucer's growing mastery of English expression; for the prose is not always by any means indifferent, or even bad, nor is the verse invariably a great step forward.

When *Boece* has been considered as a translation, scholars have frequently claimed that Chaucer's composition is simply indicative of the "standards of the day." Thus, F. N. Robinson (1957:320): "But in passing judgment upon a work of this sort [i.e., *Boece*] one should remember that literal accuracy rather than stylistic excellence was a recognized ideal of translation in

Chaucer's day." Conversely, Krapp (1915:10) maintains that *Boece* "is by no means a literal translation, such not being the standards of the day." And Gardner (1977:xvi) claims that *Boece* is "a superb scholarly work by the standards of the day." The "standards of the day," as was indicated above, are illusionary, for they encompassed everything from the *Troilus*, which is not at all a translation in the modern sense of the word, to the first Wycliffite Bible, which is little more than a literal gloss, to Trevisa's translation of *De Proprietatibus Rerum*, which is a close translation but decidedly acceptable English at the same time. Even these categories are misleading, however, for, as was also noted above, medieval translation theory and practice in general are still insufficiently understood. Jefferson (1917) and Cline (1928) are the only critics who have actually discussed Chaucer's translation technique in *Boece*; while each study is insightful and important, Chaucer's translation technique, as will become clear, is more varied and subtle than either suggests.

The present study, then, is offered as a contribution towards the evaluation of Chaucer as translator and of medieval English translation in general. *Boece* serves as a particularly good introduction to Chaucer as translator for a number of reasons: its manuscript sources have been identified with more certainty than have those of Chaucer's other translations; it is the longest of Chaucer's translations, so that it offers ample opportunity for studying his various techniques; it has never before been adequately described; and it is, as I hope to show, a work which is greatly misunderstood and underestimated. This book will primarily attempt to answer the questions "What is the origin of Chaucer's lexicon and syntax? How did he use them? And to what end?" In short, "What kind of translation is *Boece*?" An understanding of Chaucer's procedure in *Boece* will provide insights into Chaucer's own conception of translation — which, as was noted at the beginning of this chapter, is not immediately apparent — and thus may enable us to evaluate his other translations more authoritatively. The analysis here will concentrate on three major aspects of Chaucer's translation technique: the words he uses to translate his sources; the way he expresses in English the syntax of his sources; and the larger stylistic devices he uses in arranging and presenting his translation.

It should be noted, finally, that in a translation, perhaps more so than in an original composition, a writer's sensitivity to language is of primary importance: he requires a philologist's awareness of the lexicon, syntax and grammatical nuances of both his own language and the language of his source. Meaning is a translator's final objective, and understanding and mastery of language are the means to that objective. Indeed, a description of the technique of a translation is also a description of its artistry, for in any translation the artistry of the translator lies in the way he responds to his sources. In this regard, J. R. R. Tolkien's characteristically insightful but imaginative observation which prefaces this chapter is of importance. In the case of *Boece* Chaucer would, I think, "chiefly esteem the efforts to recover the detail of what he wrote... to make certain what it meant," for perhaps no other composition allowed Chaucer such opportunity to utilize his knowledge of and interest in language, and in perhaps no other work has what Chaucer meant been examined so little.[18]

CHAPTER 2

WORDS

> Ye knowe ek that in forme of speche is chaunge
> Withinne a thousand yeer, and wordes tho
> That hadden pris, now wonder nyce and straunge
> Us thinketh hem, and yet thei spake hem so,
> And spedde as wel in love as men now do;
> Ek for to wynnen love in sondry ages,
> In sondry londes, sondry ben usages.
> (*TC*.2.22-28)

It is appropriate to begin a study of Chaucer's translation technique in *Boece* with an analysis of the words he uses to translate the *Consolation*, for words, along with morphemes, are the most basic units of meaning in any work. All languages, of course, have their own peculiar structural features, and the semantic range of individual words in a given language may differ considerably from the semantic range of words in another language. Moreover, the ramifications of context and connotation — if these can be separated from semantic range — may vary from language to language. A translator's primary problem, then, is to match the words of his original with words in his own language which have similar semantic ranges and connotations. This is no small problem. In some cases, solutions may be obvious enough, such as translating German "Buch" with English "book" or French "chevalier" with English "knight." Most cases, however, are scarcely so simple, and the Bible offers many well-known examples of such translation problems. For example, the apostle John begins his gospel with Εν ἀρχῃ ἦν ὁ λόγος, which St. Jerome renders as "In principio erat uerbum."

The translators of the King James Bible, indeed all English translators of the Bible, follow St. Jerome's decision and translate the last word in the clause with "word," which is one of the meanings of λόγος. But "word" is not its only meaning; λόγος can also mean "speech," "principle" and "reason," both simply and in the Platonic sense of the "reason" which is the ordering principle on which the κόσμος is organized. Latin "uerbum" and English "word," of course, neither denote nor connote any of these meanings. In some cases, and perhaps this is one, it is not necessary that a translator use a word with the same semantic range of the word he is translating. In others, it is. A translator's success or failure, then, finally rests on his solutions, in accordance with the purpose of his translation, to such lexical problems.

In the case of *Boece*, Chaucer's vocabulary is perhaps most responsible for the frequently hostile critical reception of the translation. Jefferson (1917:26), one of the most favorable critics, describes its lexicon as simply "Latinate," while Brewer (1953:64) voices the opinion of perhaps the majority of scholars when he suggests that "at times [Chaucer] is so anxiously literal as to be almost incomprehensible." The lexicon of *Boece* does indeed contain foreign and unusual words, and Chaucer is at times "anxiously literal." But these are not necessarily bad features. If Chaucer's objective was to translate literally — "a literis" — one should not criticize him for it. And if the lexicon of *Boece* strikes the modern reader as exotic, he should not presume that it would have seemed so to Chaucer and his contemporaries as well; or if it did seem exotic, that this was not one of Chaucer's intentions. In other words, one cannot evaluate *a priori* any given translation technique, for in assessing the success of any translation, one needs to consider the objectives of the translator and the linguistic milieu in which the translation was produced.

Since Chaucer does not preface *Boece* with a statement of what his objectives are, one must infer them from what he has produced. Inference, if it is not applied rigorously, can be a tricky if not wilful business. But if all of Chaucer's translation techniques combine in a coherent pattern, one is justified in inferring the end to which these techniques were directed. While considering Chaucer's techniques, however, one needs also to consider the tradition from which those techniques arose. Although, as I suggested in the first chapter, medieval English translation techniques in general are still insufficiently understood, there are aids to the understanding of the tradition of translating individual words in the Middle Ages. These aids are the various Latin-English wordlists compiled in the fourteenth, fifteenth and sixteenth centuries, which indicate what many of Chaucer's contemporaries regarded as the appropriate translation of a given Latin word. But the wordlists, particularly the later ones, must be used with caution. One cannot presume that Chaucer had access to early versions of them. One can presume, however, if one or more of the wordlists translates a given Latin word in a certain way, that there was a "tradition" of translation for that word. It is against this tradition, in part, that any medieval English translation should be judged. If Chaucer concurs with this tradition, one ought not to make positive or negative judgments about the words he uses to translate the Latin; rather, one must simply recognize that his translation accords with the (allusive) standards of the day.[1] The wordlists which have been used for corroborative evidence in this study are: the *Medulla Grammatice* (c. 1460), and the *Ortus Vocabulorum* (c. 1500), both Latin-English lists, and the *Promptorium Parvulorum* (c. 1440) and the *Catholicon Anglicum* (c. 1483), both English-Latin lists.[2]

The objective of this chapter, then, is to determine and analyze the range, effectiveness and implications of the lexicon of *Boece*. In order to do so, individual words will be discussed in relation to the techniques of translation which obtain in *Boece* and in relation to the traditions of translation found in the various medieval wordlists. Within these relations one sees Chaucer utilizing a wide range of lexical techniques in responding to the problems of meaning in his French and Latin sources. These techniques may be divided into three general types: the substitution of native words for source words; circumlocutory ways of expressing source words; and the adoption of source words in his own language.

The substitution of native, or current, words is the most common lexical translation technique in *Boece*. Native or current words are here defined as those words which are recorded in English by 1350, thirty years before *Boece* was probably written. The predictable cases—those translations which accord with general understanding of Latin or French—are perhaps the least interesting. Such translations as "sterres" for "sidera," "glorie" for "gloria," "it nys nat leveful to hem" for "il ne leur loist pas" and "understand" for "entent" are of the sort which any competent English translator would be expected to produce. The importance of such expected translations in *Boece* lies in the fact that they occur much more frequently than the apparently inexplicable mistranslations of relatively straightforward Latin and French words. It is somewhat deceptive to compile lists of Chaucer's translational "inaccuracies," as others have done (Skeat, 1900:xxiv-vi, Fehlauer, 1909:41-45 and Jefferson, 1917:16-24). Some of the items in such lists are actual mistranslations, but others may be due to erroneous textual readings in Chaucer's manuscript sources or to fourteenth-century standards of translation. Moreover, to highlight Chaucer's "inaccuracies" is to present a distorted description of his competence as a translator. In order to offer a just picture of his competence, one should pair a list of his "inaccuracies" with a list of his correct translations. Indeed, the overall accuracy of the translation is what must be judged, and in these terms Chaucer's obvious and unwarranted mistakes must be considered minimal.

Chaucer's use of native words falls into four classifications: predictable translations (mentioned above), unpredictable translations, calques and idioms. In many cases, what the modern critic would consider predictable translations are confirmed by the Latin-English wordlists. Such confirmation reveals the soundness of the lexical translation tradition of late medieval England and demonstrates that Chaucer was clearly working within this tradition. For example, at 1m5.44 Chaucer translates "periuria" (37) and "perjurement" (26) with "forswerynge"; the *Medulla* (515) translates "periuro" with "to forswere." Similarly, at 2p3.59-60 Chaucer translates "exspectationem" (29), which Jean omits, with "abydynge"; the *Medulla* (231) pairs "exspecto" with "to abide." At 3p5.65 "ben conseyled" corresponds to "conciliat" (35) and "sont acordé" (37); the *Medulla* (152) defines "concilio" as "to Cownseyle." One more example will suffice: at 4m3.17 "godhede" translates "numen" (18) and "diex" (8). The *Medulla* (442) defines "numen" as "godhed."

The unpredictable translations, however, the translations which strike the modern reader as infelicitous, awkward or incorrect, are more interesting than the predictable ones; for these translations provide valuable insights into Middle English and medieval Latin semantics. Indeed, they demonstrate strikingly how much word morphology and the meanings of individual words have changed between the Middle Ages and the present. As Chaucer himself says at the beginning of the second book of *Troilus*, there is change in the forms of speech, and words which seem odd today were perfectly acceptable a thousand (or 600) years ago. For example, the adjectival suffix "-able" can lead the modern reader to hasty conclusions. In Old French, whence the suffix had its greatest effect on English, "-able" can have either an active or a passive meaning. Whereas in Middle English this same semantic diversity obtains, in Modern English "-able" is limited to the passive sense. Thus, the modern reader coming upon "desceyvable opynioun" (5p3.102) as a translation of "opinio fallax" (52) and "opinion decevable" (59) might presume that Chaucer has erred; in Modern English a "deceivable opinion" is an opinion which is able to be deceived. Yet the primary sense of "deceivable," the sense common in Middle English, is in fact an active sense, just as it is in Old French—"having the quality or habit of deceiving" (*MED*, s. v.). A similar word is "purveiable" (3m2.5) for "prouida" (3) and "puissant et pourveable" (2). Chaucer's "the cours unforseyn and unwar" (5p1.77) illustrates a related semantic problem; in Modern English "unware" or "unaware" has an active meaning, referring to the alertness of the person described by it. As a translation of the second adjective in "inprouisus inopinatusque concursus" (39-40) and "li cours et li assemblemens despourveuz et non-cuidiéz" (42-43), however, "unwar" clearly must have a passive meaning, referring to the fact that the "cours" is not expected. Such a definition is in fact entirely acceptable in Middle English; although the *OED* cites this passage as the first occurrence of this sense, the usage is recorded elsewhere in Chaucer and on into the fifteenth century (*OED*, s. v. sense 3).

Chaucer's "envyrounynge of the universite" (5p4.165-66) involves another word which might seem a mistranslation to a modern reader. Today, of course, "university" is limited to the sense "institution of higher learning," a sense recorded as early as 1300. But another sense common in Middle English, a sense first recorded here but found as late as the sixteenth century, is "the whole of something" (*OED*, s. v. sense 2.b), and thus Chaucer's phrase is an appropriate translation of "uniuersitatis ambitum" (79) and "l'avironnement de la communité" (90-91). The idiom in "they bare me on hande, and lieden" (1p4.251-52) is indicative of those words and phrases which seem more impenetrable than unusual. The latter part of the doublet is certainly a good translation of "mentiti sunt" (118-19) and "il me mistrent assus et mentirent" (134), while the first part seems simply odd. But the idiom "bear in hand," which Chaucer himself uses elsewhere (*CT*.III.226), is recorded as early as 1300 and as late as the eighteenth century and means "to charge or accuse," frequently with the connotation "falsely" (*OED*, s. v. "bear" v.[1] sense 3.e). Thus, Chaucer's doublet simply pairs formal and idiomatic expressions of the same idea.

The Latin-English wordlists explain several of Chaucer's other translations which might seem odd or incorrect to the modern reader. One such word, confirmed by both the wordlists and

Middle English usage in general, is "mermaydenes" (1p1.68), which translates "Sirenes" (34) and "Sereines" (37). The *Medulla* (644) defines "Siren" as "a mermayd," while both the *Promptorium* (286) and the *Catholicon* (236) define "mermaydyn" as "Siren." Moreover, mermaids and sirens were equated throughout the fourteenth and fifteenth centuries (cf. *CT*.VII. 3269-70).[3] Chaucer's use of "noryssynges" at 4p6.36 to translate "oblectamenta" (15) — the French has a loose paraphrase — might seem odd, yet the *Medulla* (447) and the *Ortus* confirm the usage by pairing "oblectamentum" with "solacium" and "leuamen." Chaucer's "noryssynge" at 1p6.84 and Jean's "norrissement"(48) also appear to be incorrect translations of "fomitem"(44), and indeed Jefferson (1917:18) lists this passage as one of Chaucer's inaccuracies in translation. But in the *Medulla* (251), "fomes" is translated by "Norysshyng." Similarly, at 4m2.17 most *Boece* manuscripts read "tyranyes" as the translation of "tyrannos"(9) and "tyrans"(9); B.M. MS Add. 10340 and Salisbury MS 113 read "tyrauntis," which Robinson (1957:905) suggests is "perhaps" correct. However, the *Medulla* (708) in fact defines "tyrannus" as "a tyranne." The phrase "whan I have first ispendid and answered"(5p4.21-22), a translation of "si prius...expendero" (9-10) and "quant je auré premierement respondu"(10-11), will serve as a final example of the importance of interpreting Chaucer's translations within the lexical milieu in which they were produced. Here, "expendero" is clearly being used in the figurative sense "to judge" or "to consider," and Middle English "answered" and Old French "respondu," if not exact translations, at least border on the semantic range of this figurative sense. However, "ispendid" seems to be an odd translation, for in Middle English and elsewhere in Chaucer's works "spend" regularly means "to dispose of," "to employ" or "to use up" (*OED*, s. v. "spend" v.[1]). "Spend" is never recorded as an intransitive verb in the figurative sense "to judge" or "to consider." Yet the various wordlists clearly show that "spend" was an acceptable translation of "expendo": the *Medulla* (231) translates "exspendo" with "to spende," while the *Promptorium* (462) and the *Catholicon* (353) translate "spendyn" with "expendo."

The wordlists very likely refer only to the literal sense of "expendo," but in any event Chaucer's "ispendid," which he perhaps used because it is a derivative of the Latin, is within the translation tradition of the lists and, even if it strikes the modern reader as odd, cannot be considered a mistranslation.

In short, while there are indeed unusual words in *Boece*—and they serve an important function, which will be discussed at the end of this chapter and in Chapter Six—the majority of the roughly 60,000 words in the translation are unexceptionable within the lexical milieu in which they were produced. The wordlists are especially important for evaluating Chaucer's lexical selection. Indeed, they constitute a relatively untapped resource, and it finally will prove more insightful to find out what they can reveal about medieval translation than simply to itemize the mistakes in any given translation.

Calques constitute another type of native word Chaucer uses to translate words in his source texts. In a calque, Theodora Bynon (1977:232) explains,

> the form and meaning of a foreign word, instead of being carried over into the recipient language as a unit, is merely employed as a model for a native creation. For this to be possible it must be both morphologically complex and semantically transparent, and the process consists in substituting for each of its morphs the semantically closest morph in the recipient language and combining these according to its own native rules of word-formation.

The use of calques demonstrates a translator's special awareness of the meaning of the words in his source; the breakdown of a source word to its elements and the replacement of those elements with equivalent elements in his own language reflects both a sensitivity to the construction of words and a concern with meaning on the part of the translator. As the Latin-English wordlists indicate, there was a tradition of using calques in medieval England, and on many occasions one sees Chaucer working with this tradition. Frequently, Chaucer's use of a calque is explained by both the wordlists and Jean's translation. For example, at 1p4.102 Chaucer translates "opposui" (44) and "je me contremis" (53) with "I putte me ayens." The *Medulla* (469) defines "oppono" as "contra ponere," and the *Ortus* defines it as "contra ponere... to put agayn" — "put" corresponding to Latin "pono" and "agayn" to Latin "op" (< "ob"), meaning "against" here. Similarly, at 2p1.78-79 Chaucer translates "retineri" (38) and "estre retenue" (43) with "ben withholden." The *Promptorium* (545) pairs "with-holdyn" with "retineo" — "holdyn" corresponding to "tineo" (< "teneo") and "wyth," meaning "back," to "re." Even when Jean does not employ a calque, Chaucer can be seen working within the tradition suggested by the wordlists. For instance, at 4p6.224 Chaucer translates "ignorantes" (111) and "cil qui en sont ignorant" (124) with "unknowynge folk"; the *Medulla* (291), breaking the Latin down to its elements, defines "ignoro" as "to vnknow." Chaucer's ability to adapt the calques suggested by the tradition is also illustrated by "forwytere" (5p6.295), one of Chaucer's neologisms in *Boece* and corresponding to "praescius" (148) and "cognisseur" (168); the *Medulla* (542) pairs "praescius" with "for Wetynte," a Southern dialectal variant of "wytynge,"[4] and thus Chaucer has created a calque on the Latin but turned his word into a noun on the model of the French.

Chaucer also creates calques which are not suggested by the wordlists. In these cases, the wordlists either do not contain the Latin word or do not translate it with a calque. As with the calques suggested by the wordlists, some of these calques may have been created on the model of Jean's translation. For instance, "withdrawe" (2p2.23) translates "retrahere" (12) and "retraire" (14). "Withdrawe" and "retraire" are clearly created on the model of translating "retineri" with "withholden" and "retenue," but both the *Promptorium* (545) and the *Catholicon* (421) define "withdrawen" as "subtraho." A similar use of "with" in the sense "against" obtains in "be withseid" (3p10.64), translating "contra dici" (34) and "estre contredit" (35-36). The prefix "to" in a separative sense, like Latin and French "de," appears in "todrawen" (4m3.43), corresponding to "detrahunt" (36) and "detraient et abessent" (20). The prefix "again," equivalent to Latin and French "re" in the sense "backward," obtains in "ayenledynge fyr" (3m9.38), translating "reduci...igne" (21) and "remenable amour" (22-23) — "amour" being one of Jean's interpretive translations. Finally, Chaucer creates many calques with "un" and "mys" corresponding to a variety of negative prefixes in Latin and French: "unknowable" (2m7.25), "ignorabiles" (21), "mescognoissable" (14); "mysknowynge" (2p8.25), "ignaram" (12), "mescognoissant" (15); "unwrappen" (4p6.2), "euoluere" (2), "desveloper" (1); "unforseyn" (5p1.77), "inprouisus" (39-40), "despourveuz" (43).

Chaucer's understanding of the construction of calques is best illustrated by the ones he creates without the assistance of Jean or the wordlist tradition. Many of these calques follow patterns discussed earlier; thus, it is clear that for Chaucer the creation of calques was a productive aspect of his lexical selection. For example, the prefix "with" appears again in "withseide" (5p1.45), a calque on Jean's "contredeist" (25) and corresponding to "refragatus est" (23-24). Chaucer's comprehension of the elements of French words also appears in "hadde thurw-perced" (3p1.2), translating "defixerat" (2-3) and "m'avoit...trespercié" (1-2), in "thurw-passen" (4m3.45), translating "penitus meant" (37) and "trespassent" (22), and in "ben put undir" (4p6.107-8), translating "subsunt" (53) and "sont sommisez" (59-60). His comprehension of the elements of Latin words appears in "unfooldeth" (4m5.7-8), translating "explicet" (5) and "face" (4).

Both Chaucer and Jean seem to have experienced considerable difficulty in translating Latin idioms and idiomatic language into their own native languages. The reasons for this are clear. First, idioms are rather complex expressions, the meanings of which frequently have little semantic overlap with what the words of the idioms actually denote. This is not to suggest that Jean and Chaucer were inadequate Latinists; their competence is revealed throughout their respective translations. Rather, any translator, no matter how competent, cannot be expected to understand an idiom he has never seen before. A second cause of the difficulty Chaucer in particular faced is suggested by the fact that the wordlists contain few idioms. Whereas medieval translators certainly confronted and correctly translated many idioms every day, the fact that idioms are not common in the wordlists perhaps indicates that their place was not firmly established in the medieval English translation tradition.

Given this inadequate background in the translation of idioms, Chaucer generally follows his most logical option: he copies Jean's translation. It is Chaucer's most logical option because, unless he knew for a fact that Jean's translation was wrong, following the French saved Chaucer the trouble of trying to interpret a construction which Jean, correctly or incorrectly, had already unraveled. Jean, of course, had two ways of treating an idiom: to translate it literally, or to attempt to express its real meaning in more natural French. In some cases, the meaning of Jean's (and Chaucer's) literal translation is clear enough. For instance, "perditum ire uoluisse" (1p4.93-94) is rendered as "aient voulu aler destruire" (108) by Jean and as "han wilned to gon destroyen" (205) by Chaucer. Similarly, Jean translates "tui causa" (3p1.19) as "pour la cause de toy" (24) and Chaucer as "for the cause of the" (43-44). On many occasions, however, the Latin idiom literally rendered in French and English makes little sense. Thus, "alieni aeris necessitate" (1p4.50) is translated by Jean as "par la necessité de l'estrange avoir" (59-60) and by Chaucer as "for nede of foreyne money" (115). The Latin idiom "aes alienum" means "the sum owed, a debt" (Lewis and Short, s. v. "aes" sense II.B.1)—and thus the Latin here should be translated as "by necessity of the debt"—while the meanings of Jean's and Chaucer's translations, *literally* constructed on the Latin, are cryptic at best.[5] Boethius's "maiestatis reum" (1p4.64) presents a similar problem. Jean translates the phrase as "coupable... contre la majesté du roy" (76-77) and Chaucer as "gylty ayens the kynges real majeste" (146). Latin "majestas" here means "the sovereignty of the people" (Lewis and Short, s. v. sense I.2), and so a person who is guilty ("reus") against the "majestas" is a person guilty of treason. However, neither Old French "majesté" nor Middle English "majeste" is recorded in the sense "the sovereignty of the people"; these words are generally used in the sense "grandeur," whether it be the Heavenly King's or an earthly king's. Rather than presume that Jean and Chaucer are using their words in extended senses, one must conclude that their literal translations have obscured the meaning of the idiom, which they very likely did not understand.

Not surprisingly, the idiomatic expressions which Jean and Chaucer do not translate literally but render in more natural language tend to have meanings which are more transparent than those of the idioms just discussed. Thus, "sed est pudori degener sanguis" (2p4.40), which literally means, "but he, ignoble in blood, is in shame," is translated by Jean as "mais il a honte de son bas lignage" (46) and by Chaucer as "but he is aschamed of his ungentil lynage" (79-80). And "cum dederit impatientiae manus" (2p4.56-57), which literally means "when he has given his hands to impatience," is translated by Jean as "quant il a perdu pacience" (66) and by Chaucer as "whan he hath lost pacience" (117-18). In his treatment of "est ubique gentium" (2p5.13), which literally means "there is of peoples anywhere," Chaucer even tightens and improves Jean's translation: "that is overal in the world" (24) as opposed to "que toutez les gens du monde ont" (15).

When he does differ from Jean in his treatment of idiomatic expressions, Chaucer may also make either a literal or a more naturalized translation. At 2p4.66 the Latin "tui compos fueris" is transparent enough, and Jean's wordy "tu es bien et resonnablement ordeneur de toy" (77-78) seems unneccessary. Chaucer, the only writer recorded for the phrase "mighty over" [*MED*, s. v. "mighti" sense 1.(e)], responds to the Latin with the literal, yet somehow equally idiomatic, "thow are myghty over thyself" (135). But few of Chaucer's literal translations of idioms are so felicitous. At 5p1.29-30 he produces "that manere wol I don the" for "Morem . . . geram tibi" (16), which actually means "I shall humor you" (Lewis and Short, s. v. "mos" sense I), even though Jean's "Ce te ferai je voulentiers" (18) expresses the Latin rather well. The idiom "nescio quem" (3p7.11-12) is perhaps particularly difficult; it is a phrase meaning "I do not know whom" but functions as a pronoun meaning "someone." In characteristic fashion, Jean alters the phrase by adding an interpretive noun: "ne sai quiex peres" (12). Chaucer, however, in equally characteristic fashion, attempts a literal translation of the idiom. His "I not how manye" (20-21) is a result of either the substitution in his Latin manuscript of "quam" for "quem" or of his misreading of the common, and similar, abbreviations of "quem," "quam," and "quantum" (see Cappelli, 1960:303); it should be noted, however, that in C.U.L. MS Ii.3.21 "quem" is usually abbreviated as "quē."

One might argue that idioms are the touchstones of a good translator, so that Jean's and Chaucer's difficulties with them indicate serious deficiencies in their competence as Latinists. Yet the linguistic milieu in which they wrote must, again, be considered. Barring idioms, Jean's and Chaucer's translations are generally quite accurate, and so their difficulties with idioms, in conjunction with the relative absence of idioms in the wordlists, may indicate that the translation of idioms was in general uncertain in the Middle Ages. A thorough examination of idioms throughout the medieval period is required. In any event, the awkwardness of many of Chaucer's translations is due to the fact that, perhaps not aware of the extrapolated meaning of an idiom, he frequently attempted a literal translation. While not always wrong, such translations are typically infelicitous. Indeed, Chaucer's treatment of Latin idioms which he does not attempt to express literally is frequently very good. For instance, Chaucer responds to "Cur ita prouenit" (2p6.55), which Jean translates as "Et pour quoy avient il ainsi" (61), with the nicely concise "And whi is it thus" (110). And "it nis no resoun" (4p4.291), translating "ratione caret" (132) and "n'a point de raison" (149), has a distinctively Chaucerian tone; in the *Merchant's Tale* one finds "as skile is and reson" (*CT*.IV.1678) and in the *Squire's Tale* "as reson was" (*CT*.V.296).

There are, of course, mistakes in *Boece*, and this discussion of Chaucer's substitution of current words for source words will close with a consideration of the occasional vague or incorrect translations he has made. But rather than simply to list the mistakes, as others have done, it will be more profitable to classify them and attempt to determine what caused them. One common type of mistake does indeed arise from what Brewer has called Chaucer's "anxious literalness." For example, Chaucer translates "fama, si cum inexhausta aeternitate cogitetur" (2p7.54) with "renome...were thought to the regard of eternyte, that is unstaunchable and infynyt" (109-12). Chaucer's "were thought" is an awkwardly literal translation of "cogitetur," and Jean's rendering of the clause is clearer and more precise: "la renommee... se elle est comparee a la pardurableté qui ne puet estre espuisiee ne comprise" (59-61). Another example of Chaucer's overly literal translations is "in erthis" (4p6.368), translating "in terris" (182) and "es terrez" (202). Latin "terra" in the plural, of course, frequently means simply "the world," and Chaucer's odd translation[6] is perhaps the result of the combined influence of the French and Latin plurals. But if "in erthis" can be explained, it is difficult to account for the similar "withouten doutes" (3p11.189), translating "me indubitato" (91-92) and "sens doubter" (99-100). Although Chaucer's translation is not incorrect, this plural form of "without doubt" is not recorded in the *MED* or the *OED* and does not seem necessitated by either the Latin or the French.

The translation of French prepositions such as "de," which has a variety of meanings, seems to have caused Chaucer considerable difficulty. For instance, on several occasions Chaucer produces a vague expression by rendering "de," in the sense "of," with "to." Thus, he translates "sceleratorum...poena" (4p4.7) and "la paine des cruex hommes" (8) with "the peyne to shrewes" (16). Although one can interpret "to" as meaning "with respect to," the frequency of the usage in *Boece* suggests that Chaucer simply misunderstood the French. Indeed, Chaucer frequently translates French "de" imprecisely. At 2p7.48 "in largesse and in greet doynge" corresponds to "amplum magnificumque" (20) and "de grandeur et de largeur" (23); the vagueness of Chaucer's phrase is due to his awkward imitation of the idiomatic French treatment of the Latin direct objects. In the following example Chaucer creates confusion by editing the French:

> Vestes erant tenuissimis filis subtili artificio indissolubili materia perfectae (1p1.12-13)

> Ses robes estoient de tres deliéz filz et de soutille ourvaingne, de matiere pardurable parfetes (11-12)
> Hir clothes weren makid of right delye thredes and subtil craft, of perdurable matere (19-21)

Here, Jean uses "de," meaning "out of," to introduce source clauses corresponding to the Latin ablatives. Chaucer's "of" is thus an appropriate translation of "de," for "of," too, can indicate the material of which something is made. But, despite Robinson's punctuation, the omission of "of" before "subtil craft" results in the prepositional phrase "of perdurable matere" modifying "subtil craft" and thus destroys the parallelism of both Boethius's and Jean's sentences.

A third type of Chaucer's mistakes results, quite simply, from the difficulty of the Latin. In many cases Jean also mistranslates the passage. For example, at 1p4.218 Chaucer renders "quanta mei periculi securitate" (99-100) and "par com grant suerté de mon peril" (116) with "with how gret sykernesse of peril." Normally, "securitas" means "security," and "sekernes" is how the *Medulla* (624) defines it. Here, however, "securitas" is being used in the rather unusual sense "heedlessness" (Lewis and Short, s. v. sense I.B); that Chaucer and Jean should be unaware of this sense is not remarkable. Although one cannot conclude from the absence of a given Latin word in the wordlists that the word was unknown in the Middle Ages, one is perhaps justified in presuming that the word was not especially common. If this is the case, then a word which has a figurative meaning distinct from what it literally denotes can be expected to cause medieval translators particular difficulty. Such an explanation seems to account for the following passage:

> eoque modo percurrenti cetera (3p11.34-35)
> Et qui voudroit ainsi corre par toutez ces autrez chosez (35-36)
> And whoso wolde renne in the same manere be alle thinges (68-70)

Latin "percurro," which literally means "to run through," is not listed in either the *Medulla* or the *Ortus*. Jean's "corre par" is a literal translation of the Latin, but Chaucer's "renne...be"

25

indicates that he misread "par" as an instrumental. In any event, both Jean's and Chaucer's translations are incorrect as well as vague, for here "percurro" has the rather distantly removed figurative sense "to scan" (Lewis and Short, s. v. sense I.B.3).[7]

Finally, it should be noted that there are indeed vague and awkward passages in *Boece* which have no apparent explanation. For instance, Chaucer translates "suppetunt" (2p4.24) and "remaingnent" (28) with "ben...dwelled" (48). Although this is the earliest citation in the *MED* of the use of "dwell" with an abstract noun [s. v. sense 8.(a)], the real problem with Chaucer's translation is that he uses "dwell" in the passive voice; this usage is not recorded elsewhere, is difficult to interpret, and seems an odd response to the active Latin and French verbs. As a translation of "repetit" (3p2.46) and "requiert" (48), "reherceth and seketh" (84) is another inexplicably odd translation. Although "reherceth" is an acceptable translation of "repetit," in this passage, which discusses man's soul's attempt to obtain "bonum suum," the Latin clearly means "seeks." English "reherceth" is not recorded in this latter sense. Nor is it ever recorded with the sense "to do something again" and in conjunction with another verb, whereby it might, in effect, modify the following verb; thus, one cannot translate Chaucer's doublet with "repeatedly seeks." But before examining the implications of the techniques described in this section, it will be best to consider the two other general ways in which Chaucer treats his sources.

When two languages differ in structure as much as Latin and English do, periphrasis, which includes the use of doublets, is almost a necessary translation technique. Many Latin words, particularly adjectives and verbs, have a semantic complexity which cannot be expressed by a single English word. In many cases this holds true for French as well, and so Chaucer, again, frequently takes the logical choice of following Jean's translations. But his creation of his own periphrases, as well as his combined translations of the Latin and French, demonstrates that periphrasis, like the use of calques, was a functional aspect of his lexical selection. Moreover, he does not simply imitate all of the French periphrases, for when he has the opportunity of employing a single word, he does so. For example, when Jean translates "constantiam" (2p3.41) with "point de estableté" (46), Chaucer responds with the simple "stedfastnesse" (82). Periphrasis, of course, can make sentences rather wordy and thus may explain why Fisher and others have found Chaucer's expression to be "fumbling." But since words like "impotence," "notify" and "triumphal" were not current in Chaucer's day, unless Chaucer created even more neologisms—and he has generally been criticized for having used too many—he had to employ periphrases. Certainly, some of his periphrases are infelicitous or unnecessary, but their meanings are always clear, and one can scarcely criticize him for that.[8]

"In" is a common prefix in Latin, and two of the simplest periphrases employed by Jean and Chaucer—when Chaucer does not substitute the native negative prefix "un"—are of the negative words thus created. In general, their periphrases consist of the prepositions "sens" and "withoute" and a noun which translates the root of the Latin word. For example:

indefensi (1p4.113)	sans deffense (129-30)	Withoute deffense (242-43)
infinitam (4p4.26)	sens fin (30)	withouten ende (56-57)
innumerabiles (4p6.7)	sens nombre (9)	withoute nombre (18)

The construction can also be employed as a translation of Latin adverbs: "inuiolabiliter" (3p10.35), "sans corruption" (38) and "withoute corrupcioun" (66-67). This type of periphrasis is concise and easily constructed, allowing Jean and Chaucer to translate any of the negative Latin words for which French and English had no one-word equivalent. Such a simple periphrasis can be an almost automatic response, and indeed on those occasions when Jean uses a different construction, Chaucer frequently uses the simpler periphrasis:

innumeri...populi (1m5.40)	tuit li peuple (28)	peple withouten nombre (49)

indiuisum (3p9.9)	ne puet estre devisee	withouten ony
	(11-12)	devysioun (17-18)

The other periphrasis of negative Latin words which Jean and Chaucer use is limited to abstract nouns. This periphrasis consists of "faute" and "defaute" and the root noun of the Latin word. For example:

impotentia (4p2.71)	faute de poissance (73)	defaute of power
		(144-45)
impunitas (4p4.60)	faute de paine (64)	defaute of peyne
		(124-25)

The simplicity of the Latin roots in such words allows for the simplicity of the periphrases; that is, since in every case French and English have a word equivalent to the Latin root, all Jean and Chaucer need do is negate the root. When the Latin root is more complex, however, expressing either two ideas or an idea for which French and English lack a one-word equivalent, the periphrases which Jean and Chaucer employ are more complex. Thus, the adjective "herbipotens" (4m3.9) expresses a relation between nouns—"qui habet herbarum potentiam"—and so Jean and Chaucer respond, respectively, with "puissant sus les herbez" (4) and "myghti over the erbes" (8). Similarly, "Pythagoricum illud" (1p4.122) refers to something which is "of Pythagoras"; the Greek quotation which the words introduce clearly indicates what "illud" is. Such a construction, however, in which a pronoun is defined by what precedes and follows it, is perhaps alien to French and English, for Jean produces "icest commandement de Pitagoras" (139) and Chaucer "thilke commaundement of Pictagoras" (260-61).

In addition to the notational complexity of the root of a Latin word, the morphology of the word can necessitate periphrasis in French and English. In short, the more notationally and morphologically complex the Latin word, the more complex the periphrasis. Latin words which consist of two or more prefixes can cause particular problems, for such structures are not an aspect of native English word formation. Although compounding was a vital part of word formation in Old English—indeed in all

Germanic languages, especially Old Icelandic—for the most part these compounds consist of adjectives and nouns; almost all the multi-prefix words in Modern English are derived, one way or another, from Latin. A characteristically complex Latin word is "inexorabiles" (1p4.26). It consists of the root "oro," meaning "to pray," the adjectival suffix "-abilis," meaning "given to" or "able to," the prefix "-ex," meaning "out of," and the negative prefix "in": "unoutprayable" or "unentreatable." Given this complexity, then, the clauses Jean and Chaucer use to translate "inexorabiles" are understandable: "qui ne pooient estre fenies par prieres" (28) and "that ne myghte nat ben relessed by preyeris" (50-51). Similar to "inexorabiles" is "inexpugnabiles" (4p6.139), which Jean translates as "Li uns qui ne porent estre vaincuz par tourmens" (155) and Chaucer as "and som men, that ne mowen nat ben overcomen by torment" (277-78).

Some words, such as "triumphalis" in "triumphali largitione" (2p3.29-30), are structurally simple but notationally complex; with the exception of its derivative "triumphal," it seems to lack a one-word equivalent in English, Middle or Modern. Thus, Chaucer, following Jean's "de si large loenge comme on seult chanter aus victores" (34), produces "with so large preysynge and laude as men syngen in victories" (61-62). Latin "reducem" is structurally and notationally simple, and, as was noted above, on one occasion Chaucer and Jean form calques on it—"ayenledynge" and "remenable." At 4m1.23, however, its usage in the clause "Huc te si reducem referat uia" complicates the translation of it. The adjectival modification of a personal pronoun is a construction which has limited currency in both Old French and Middle English. Thus, Jean and Chaucer respond to "reducem" with a clausal periphrasis: "si que tu soies la remenéz" (14) and "so that thou be brought thider" (34).

Most of the lexical periphrases which Jean and Chaucer produce are of verbs, for many of the Latin verbs which express a condition or result do not have one-word equivalents in Old French or Middle English. Jean and Chaucer respond to these verbs in two general ways. The first way is to employ "avoir" and

TECHNIQUES OF TRANSLATION

"haven" and an abstract noun which signifies the condition implicit in the Latin verb. For example:

indignemur (3p4.5)	nous avons desdaing (5)	Y have right gret disdayn (9)
erubescant (3p6.7-8)	aient honte (7)	han schame (11)
laetor (3p11.104)	trop ai grant leesce de toy (112)	I have greet gladnesse of the (217-18)
"Recte," inquit, "aestimas" (4p4.30)	"Tu en as," dist elle, "droite estimacion" (33)	"Thou hast," quod sche, "the ryght estimacion of this" (62-63)

A few common verbs, such as "impero," are almost invariably translated with this type of periphrasis:

Num quicquam... imperabis (2p6.21)	Pourras tu jamais avoir seigneurie ou commandement (26-27)	Maystow evere have any comaundement (47-48)
imperet (2m8.8)	a seignorie (4)	hath comaundement (6-7)
non imperet (3p5.10-11)	n'a point de seignorie ne de commandement (11)	ne hath ne lordschipe ne comaundement (16-17)

The other common way in which Jean and Chaucer respond to Latin verbs expressing a condition or result is with "estre" and "ben" and an adjective, noun, or prepositional phrase:

seruiat (3m5.7)	soit serve (4)	be thral (7)
inter...numerentur (3p11.15)	il soient mis au nombre (15)	thei mowen be put in the nombre (28-29)
cum discrepant (3p11.17)	quant elles sont diversez (17)	whan thei ben diverse (34-35)
subsistere (3p11.35)	est en sa sustance (36-37)	is in his substaunce (71)
Nisi quis insaniat (4p2.109-10)	s'il n'est hors de sens (118-19)	but yif he be out of his wyt (229-30)

For all of the examples just discussed, one might argue that Chaucer is not responding to the Latin but mechanically translating the French. Yet his decision to do so demonstrates his generally good eye for semantics. It is true that by so closely following Jean, Chaucer occasionally creates periphrases where his own competence should, or the tradition of the wordlists does, offer him alternatives. Thus, Chaucer might have translated "impero," noted above, with "command," a verb current in his day and listed in the *Medulla* (296) as the translation of "impero." Although the wordlists contain few periphrases — "inexorabilis" and "inexpugnabilis" do not occur in the *Medulla* — there are indications that a tradition of periphrasis did exist in the late Middle Ages; the *Ortus* translates "inexpugnabilis" with "inuincibilis not abyll to be ouercome," a periphrasis which is quite close to the one Jean and Chaucer produce. Indeed, in some cases, the periphrasis offered by the wordlists is at least as good as, if not better than, the one Chaucer creates on Jean's example; for instance, the *Ortus* translates "insanio" as "to waxe wode." But for most of the words discussed, the wordlists offer only one-word translations, many of which are less precise than Jean's and Chaucer's periphrases; in the *Ortus*, "to wene or hope" — compared to Jean's "avoir droite estimacion" and Chaucer's "han the ryght estimacion" — is paired with "aestimo." Moreover, many of the periphrases that the wordlists do contain are only slightly closer to natural English than the single Latin word they translate — "inexorabilis" is translated by "non exorabilis... qui nullius precibus flectitur" in the *Ortus*. In such cases Chaucer's decision to follow Jean's periphrasis rather than what may have been commonly regarded as an acceptable English translation demonstrates, if not his originality, then his sensitivity to meaning. Yet when Jean is able to translate a single Latin word with a single French one, and there is no one-word English equivalent, Chaucer's translation is frequently in harmony with the tradition of the wordlists. For example, Chaucer renders "attenuare" (1p6.52) and "atenuraier" (56) with "to maken thynne and wayk" (98-99); the *Medulla* (55) translates "attenuo" as "to make thynne" and the *Ortus* as "to make thyne or febule." But it is clear that Chaucer could, if need be, create his own periphrases, such as "mowen waxen esy and softe" (1p5.76) for "mollescant" (38) and "se amolissent" (40); both the *Medulla* and the *Ortus* render "mollesco" inexactly.[9] Chaucer's

31

proficiency in periphrasis is also demonstrated by "the sighte... was in ydel" (1p1.19) as a translation of "[quae] frustrabatur intuitum" (11), which Jean renders with "[elle] decevoit la veue" (10-11). Thus, although many of the periphrases Chaucer uses may not be original creations, his use of them reveals his proficiency and understanding of the technique. Where the French offered him the best periphrasis, he followed it; where the translation tradition in which he was writing offered the best periphrasis, he followed it; and where neither the French nor the tradition were exact enough, he created his own periphrases.

This proficiency is also apparent in Chaucer's periphrastic treatment of certain semantically "loaded" Latin adjectives and adverbs. Words such as "alterum" and "quouis" are common in any Latin work, and their meaning cannot be considered complex. Yet because of the precise relationships they indicate, the translation of them can at times be difficult. In such cases Chaucer, again, frequently takes the logical choice; rather than try to unravel the words and their relationships himself, he follows Jean's example. For instance:

Quouis iudice (2p2.4)	devant quelconques juge que tu voudras (5-6)	byforn what juge that thow wolt (7-8)
in alterum (2p5.11)	de l'un a l'autre (11)	fro o man to an othir (18-19)
quocumque (4m1.13)	en touz les lieus ou (7-8)	in alle the places there as (18)
In utroque (5p3.32)	en l'un et en l'autre (40)	in the toon and in the tothir (60-61)

That Chaucer is in fact aware of the Latin meaning and not simply following the French is clear from the instances where he eliminates or alters unnecessary French words. For instance, he eliminates "semblable" in the following:

| hinc (5p4.41) | par ce semblable que je te dirai (49) | by this that I schal seyn (86) |

The combined translation of the Latin original and French translation is by nature a technique for which Chaucer alone is responsible in *Boece*. He uses the technique in a variety of ways and for a variety of purposes, but the discussion here will focus on only the combined translations of individual words. Like periphrasis, combined translation is a circumlocutory technique — it is a way of speaking around the meaning implicit in the Latin and French where a translation of the Latin or French word alone would not cover the same semantic range. Chaucer's philological skill is apparent in the way he combines the two translations so that the "seams" do not show.

In the simplest examples of combined translation, the words Chaucer employs are the same part of speech as the words they translate. In some cases the French word is also the same part of speech as the Latin but clarifies the Latin or expresses a figurative meaning implicit in it. For example:

fratris [i.e. Apollo] (1m5.6)	du solail (4)	of the sonne hir brothir (7-8)
tenues...nexus (5m3.10)	les soutilz enlacemens (9)	the thynne subtile knyttynges (16-17)

In other cases, although there frequently is no obvious semantic difference between the French and Latin, they do involve different structures or parts of speech, which Chaucer retains in his translation:

flagitiosum (1p4.146)	chascun tourmenteur (166)	every luxurious turmentour (312)[10]
domum (3p2.47)	a son ostel (51)	hom to his hous (88)
Cadit Hesperias...in undas (3m2.31)	chiet au vespre et semble qu'il se couche es ondes de la mer (22)	that falleth at even in the westrene wawes (36-37)
regia potestas (3p5.24)	la puissance des roys (27)	the real power of kynges (45)
Papae (4p2.1)	Trop me merveil et sui tous eshabiz (1)	Owh! I wondre me (1)

Many combined translations involve alteration of the original parts of speech. Such alterations suggest not only the broad comprehension Chaucer had of both the meaning and structure of Latin and French words, but also his ability to manipulate his

33

native vocabulary towards a desired end. Although there frequently are semantic differences between the Latin and French, in some cases the alteration of the words seems to be the "raison d'être" of the combined translations. One of the most common of such translations involves turning a French noun which translates a Latin noun into an adjective which modifies the English translation of the Latin noun:

in hoc uitae salo (1p3.22)	en ceste amertume de vie (32-33)	in the byttere see of this lif (63-64)
uoluptate (3p2.32)	de deliz corporex (23)	in voluptuous delyt (43)
nefas (3p10.49)	felonnie (52)	felenous cursydnesse (94-95)[11]

In the second example, of course, it is the Latin noun which is turned into an adjective.

French nouns which translate nouns may also be left as such but placed in prepositional phrases modifying an English translation of the Latin noun. For example:

ualidioribus haustibus (2p1.18)	plus fors medecines (22)	strengere drynkes of medycines (39-40)

In the following example, just the opposite holds true, with the Latin noun being used in a prepositonal phrase modifying the French abstraction of it:

fidibus lentis (3m2.6)	par sons delitables (1)	with slakke and delytable sown of strenges (1-2)

In a final example of combined translation, Chaucer takes the noun of a French prepositional phrase, which translates a Latin adjective, and turns it back into an adjective:

praeclara potentia (3p5.5)	moult est ore puissance de grant noblece (5-6)	a noble thyng and a cleer thyng is power (7-8)

As was suggested above, the very act of manipulating Latin, French and English words in this way seems to have appealed to Chaucer as much as the semantic clarification thus obtained. A full discussion of this argument will be left for the end of this chapter, where all the evidence may be collected. For the present, it will have to suffice to note that this manipulation of language—this exploration of the ways words can be restructured—suggests the joy Chaucer had in language as language. Phrases such as "the real power of kynges" justifiably strike the modern reader as redundant, while phrases such as "with slakke and delytable sown of strenges" perhaps strike him as nicely responsive to the Latin. Yet the phrases merit further consideration. The redundancy of the former phrase does indeed distinguish it from the latter, but Chaucer created them in the same way—by manipulating language. If one is content simply to regard the one as bad translation and the other as good, one misses the philological ingenuity which created both. And this philological ingenuity is so prominent, when *Boece* is compared to its sources, that it may be one of the effects Chaucer intended, if not for the average reader of the fourteenth (much less twentieth) century, then for himself.

Doublets—the translation of a single Latin or French word by two English words—constitute the final circumlocutory technique Chaucer uses in creating his lexicon. Doublets can be an effective way of capturing the semantic range of a source word and are pervasive, though generally as stylistic ornaments,[12] throughout medieval translation. Of course, as in much of Caxton's work, they can also be used excessively and indiscriminately, and most critics of *Boece* have regarded Chaucer's doublets as similarly ineffective. Thus, Lounsbury (1892:2.154) notes, "Everyone who examines carefully the poet's version of Boethius will be struck by the frequency with which a single noun or verb of the Latin is rendered into English by two which have little or no difference in their meaning."

Indeed, many of Chaucer's doublets do seem to achieve no semantic clarification. For example:

inquam (1p4.5)[13]	dis (5)	answeride and seide (8)
deplorasti (1p6.12)	pleuras (10)	bywayledest and byweptest (18-19)

haerere (2p6.41)	acompaignier (46)	cleven or joynen (87)
uultus (1p4.11)	voult (11)	my face or my chere (19-20)

In the last example, "chere," as opposed to "face," perhaps suggests "disposition" [*MED*, s. v. "chere" n.(1) sense 5.(a)], but if this is the case, the semantic distinction thus achieved does not seem particularly important. Some doublets contain one word which is a derivative of either the Latin or the French, but such doublets can still be tautological:

componebas (1p4.124)	tu ordenoies (141)	thow hast ordeyned and set (264-65)
mortales (5p6.93)	mortel (104)	mortal or dedly (181)

Jefferson (1917:37-38 and 42) lists several examples of alliterating doublets and contends that "Chaucer frequently translates each of several Latin words of a sentence by two English words not differing greatly in meaning. . . . The result is to make the sentence fuller and more impressive." Similarly, Geissman (1952:242 and 259) suggests that in general Chaucer creates doublets in his translations for style rather than as glosses on unfamiliar words, and many of the doublets which embody little semantic distinction do indeed alliterate. For example:

obduxerat (1p1.15-16)	avoit occurcie (15)	hadde duskid and dirked (26)
obstupi (1p1.41)	m'esbahi (43)	I wax al abayssched and astoned (78-79)
constet. . . nihil (2m3.18)	nulle chose. . . ne soit estable (11)	nothyng. . . nys stedfast ne stable (22-23)
sarcinulas (1p3.39)	sarpillieres (40)	sarpleris or sachelis (75)
studiis (1p1.34)	es estudes (36)	in the studies or scoles (66)

In the last two examples, one might argue, there is a semantic distinction: "sachelis" matches "sarcinulas" as meaning "small bags," and "sarpleris" matches "sarpillieres" as meaning "big bags"; and "studies" is used in the sense "application of mind to the acquisition of learning," while "scoles" refers to "the doctrine or teaching of a master"—i.e. a school of thought (*OED*, s. v. "study" sb. sense 5.a and "school" sb.¹ sense III.11). Yet, it is impossible to determine if Chaucer regarded these semantic distinctions as more important than the alliteration. Perhaps another "stylistic" doublet is "required and desired" (4p2.57-58), a translation of "desiderari" (28) and "est...desiréz" (28). Here there is a semantic distinction—although "required" is not really justified by either the Latin or the French—but Chaucer perhaps used the words simply because they rhyme.

If only the occasional desire for "style" accounts for Chaucer's doublets, it would be best to leave consideration of them, as Jefferson does, to a discussion of style. And if there is no reason, semantic of stylistic, for the doublets, it would be best to conclude that the doublets are simply some of the padding which renders Chaucer's expression "fumbling." But this would be a hasty conclusion. The origin and subtler distinctions of Chaucer's doublets must first be examined. Such an examination reveals that for Chaucer doublets could be an effective semantic—rather than just ornamental—technique.

It should first be noted that Jean's translation also abounds in doublets and that many of Chaucer's doublets are simply copied from the French. But whereas most of Chaucer's doublets do contain subtle semantic distinctions, a large number of Jean's do not; indeed, Jean's doublets, rather than Chaucer's, deserve to be labeled padding. For example:

Haud aliter (1p3.1)	Ainsi et non pas autrement (1)	Ryght so, and noon other wise (1)
exclamat (3p6.2)	s'escria...et dist (2)	cride and seide (4)
calles (3p8.31)	chemins ne sentiers (32)	weyes ne pathes (60)
fas (1p3.11)	avenant ne chose laissable (11)	nat leveful ne syttynge thyng (16-17)
exaggerat (4p5.17)	me comble et m'acrait (18)	hepith and encreseth (30)

The last two examples merit discussion. Latin "fas" could be regarded as a semantically "loaded" word—like the adjectives and adverbs for which Chaucer follows Jean's periphrastic translations—but the elements of both Chaucer's and Jean's doublets say much the same thing. In the last example, the French and English doublets achieve no semantic clarification, but it is worth noting that Chaucer's doublet consists of a native and a romance word. Such a combination is not by itself, as one might argue, very significant, if for no other reason than that one cannot assume Chaucer would have distinguished a difference in register or naturalness between Germanic words and words like "encreseth," which is recorded early in the fourteenth century. Chaucer does, however, on occasion improve the style of Jean's tautological doublets, even if he does nothing to broaden their semantic range. For instance, in the following example Chaucer improves the redundancy of Jean's doublets with alliteration— which does seem to have been one of Chaucer's minor concerns: "tristes" (3p7.6), "dolereusez et tristez" (7) and "sorweful and sorye" (12).

Of course, not all of Jean's doublets are tautological. For example, the two elements of Jean's doublets, which Chaucer imitates, may offer two acceptable translations of the Latin word they translate:

ne...exigeretur (1p4.40)	ne fust requise ne ne passast (49)	ne was nat axid ne took effect (87-88)
fortunatus (2p8.20)	richez et aesiéz et beneuréz (23)	ryche and weleful (42)

Jean and Chaucer may also employ derivatives which came to have meanings different from the Latin source. Hence, such derivatives are paired with other words which do represent the meaning of the Latin: "ad magistratum" (1p4.24), "a mestrie ne a dignité" (26) and "to maistrie or dignyte" (47). Here, Old French "mestrie" and Middle English "maistrie" mean "power," while Latin "magistratus" means "the office of a magistrate," his "dignyte."[14] In the following passage, Jean offers two acceptable translations, but Chaucer misreads the French and thus produces an inaccurate translation: "pessumdari" (1p4.35), "estre grevees et misez au desouz" (37) and "ben harmed or amenused" (70). One of the meanings of "pessumdari" is "to sink down," which

Jean renders with "misez au desouz." Chaucer, however, understands Jean's translation in a figurative sense and consequently translates it with "amenused."

Another type of Jean's doublets consists of literal and figurative translations of the Latin. In most cases, both meanings are implicit in the way Boethius uses the word, and by creating a doublet Jean (and Chaucer) marks out, as it were, the semantic boundaries of the word:

melius nitent (2p5.8-9)	resplandissent miex et rendent plus nobles et miex renomméz (8-9)	shyneth and yeveth bettre renoun (13-14)
Accipe (2p7.58)	Or reçoif et entent (65)	Have now, here, and undirstand (119-20)[15]
constituit (3p2.43)	juge...et establist (45-46)	juggid and establissyde (78-79)
deprehenditur (3p3.12-13)	est...cogneue et reprise (14)	is knowen and ataynt (22)
splendorem (3p4.41)	sa resplendisseur et son pris (45-46)	prys and shynynge (91)
esse collectum (4p2.23)	nous avons cueilli et monstré (23-24)	I have gaderid and ischewid (47-48)
lubrica (4m2.8)	escouloriable et decevable (8)	slidynge and desceyvynge (14)

Occasionally, this philological interest in the exact denotation of a word produces literal translations of Latin words which have only figurative meanings:

eo abiectior (3p4.20-21)	plus vilz et plus degitéz (22-23)	the fowlere and the more outcast (45-46)
cognitor (4p4.107)	juges...ou cognoisseur des chosez (124-25)	a juge or a knowere of thinges (235-36)

The literal meanings of "abiectior" and "cognitor" are indeed, respectively, "more cast away" and "knower"; yet the words are always used with their figurative senses, "more wretched" and "judge." Jean's doublets thus reveal that he, too, was interested in the construction of words, although, as will become clear, much less so than Chaucer.

39

TECHNIQUES OF TRANSLATION

The final type of the French doublets which Chaucer imitates consists of one word which translates the Latin and one word which expresses an extrapolation of that meaning. That is, the extrapolated word, which strictly speaking is not justified by the Latin, expresses the condition which results from what the Latin word signifies. For example: "crimen iniqui" (1m5.36), "le blasme et la paine du felon" (25) and "the blame and the peyne of the felon" (43). The "iniquus" man, because he is accused—experiences "blasme" or "crimen"—consequently suffers "paine." Similar examples are:

tranquillitatis (2p1.33)	de leesce et de pesibleté (38)	of pees and of joye (67)
error (3p9.9)	erreur et folie (12)	errour and folie (18)
inanem conceptionem (5p5.25-26)	vaine et fausse la concepcion (30)	concepcioun...veyn and fals (53-54)

It should be noted that the extrapolated word does not always follow the word which translates the Latin; thus, because one has "tranquillitas" or "pesibleté," one experiences "leesce."

In creating his own doublets, Chaucer follows these same patterns of construction. Yet his use of them, as well as his creation of new patterns, reveals a sensitivity to meaning, a skill in word formation, and a fascination with words themselves. Almost all of Chaucer's doublets involve a combination, either semantic or lexical, of the Latin and French. In the instances where Jean's translation expresses only one of the meanings implicit in the Latin, Chaucer may pair it with another acceptable meaning:

profanae (1p3.25-26)	de la fole (25)	of the wikkide or unkunnynge (48-49)
hospes (2m5.15)	hostes (8)	gest ne straunger (19)
nec ullus...modus (4p6.8)	ne nulle fins (10)	no manere ne noon ende (20-21)

It will be noted that in the second example both the Latin and the French contain the semantic range suggested by Chaucer's doublet. When the one-word French translation reflects only the figurative meaning of the Latin, Chaucer frequently supplements Jean's translation with a literal translation. In all the following examples, by chance, the literal translation is second:

margine (1p1.16)	oule (16)	hem or bordure (28)
Deprehendisti (2p1.29)	as tu cogneu (32)	Thou hast now knowen and ateynt (57)
infuderis (2p5.40)	tu y ajusteras (50)	thow wolt thresten or powren (82-83)
abiectius (3p9.26)	plus vilz et plus despite (31)	the feblere . . . or the more outcast (56-57)

In the last example, both elements of Jean's doublet express the figurative meaning of the Latin. On the occasions when the French offers a literal rather than a figurative translation, Chaucer may add the latter, which in both of the following examples is the second word:

| enatabimus (2p4.31) | nous nouerons oultre (37) | I shal wel fleetyn forth and escapyn (60-61) |
| collegimus (3p11.108) | nous avons concueilli (117) | we han gadrid and comprehendid (227-28) |

When Jean is able to match the literal and figurative meanings of the Latin with one word, Chaucer, in order to express this same semantic range, sometimes is required to create a doublet:

| refragari (3p10.57) | aler contre (60) | denye ne withstonde (110-11) |

Similar to the doublets which contain literal and figurative meanings are the doublets which consist of a translation of the Latin and a translation of the French extrapolation of it. These extrapolations may express a meaning which strictly speaking is not justified by the Latin but certainly is implicit in it or may slightly alter the Latin to a word which is more contextually appropriate in French (and English). For example:

| spinis (1p1.29) | painturez (29) | thornes and prikkynges (53) |
| deleuit oblivio (2p7.41) | sont mis en oubli (46) | put out of mynde and doon awey (86-87) |

41

premat (4m1.17)	marchera (9)	he schal pressen and wenden (25)

Chaucer's doublets may also reflect the stylistic differences between the Latin and French:

intimus (4p6.58)	plus dedens (65)	innerest or most withinne (117)
unde...uiget (5m4.16)	dont...vient (11)	whennes thryveth thanne or whennes comith (27)

The first example reveals Chaucer deciding between simple and periphrastic superlatives—a decision which continues to haunt speakers of modern English—while the second offers the "poetic" Latin and "less poetic" French ways of saying the same thing.

Chaucer's desire to represent the full semantic range of a Latin word occasionally creates problems of interpretation; for example, see his translation of "repetit" by "reherceth and seketh" (p. 26 above), where "reherceth" is clearly not a contextually appropriate meaning. Moreover, a combination of the Latin and French may result in ungrammatical structures, such as in the following passage, where Chaucer pairs present and past participles:

relictus potest (5p1.22)[16]	puet estre demourans (23)	myght ben left or duellynge (39-40)

The anacoluthon of such a translation is certainly not impenetrable, but more serious problems arise when Jean has thoroughly altered the Latin construction:

> Plurimi uero boni fructum gaudio laetitiaque metiuntur (3p2.21-22)
> Li pluseurs cuident que joie et leesche soit li souverains biens (22)
> And many folk mesuren and gessen that sovereyne good be joye and gladnesse (39-41)

Eight of the nine extant manuscripts of *Boece*,[17] as well as the editions of Caxton and Thynne, read "be joye"; C.U.L. MS Ii.3.21, one of the best manuscripts, reads "by joye," although it should be noted that "be" is a common spelling variant of "by" in

Middle English manuscripts. If "mesuren," translating "metiuntur," were the only verb Chaucer had used, "by," corresponding to the Latin ablatives, would have to be regarded as the correct reading. But if "gessen," translating "cuident," were the only verb Chaucer had used, then "be," corresponding to "soit," would have to be regarded as the correct reading. To complicate matters further, C.U.L. MS Ii.1.38, on which Robinson's text is based, reads "that the sovereyne good." The article here solves the grammatical problems, for "gessen" is commonly used in the sense "to conclude" with a clausal complement introduced by "that" [*MED*, s. v. sense 1.(b)]. However, of the manuscripts and early printed editions, only C.U.L. MS Ii.1.38 has this article, and so, on the principle of "difficilior lectio," it is most probable that not Chaucer but a scribe or editor inserted it. As the text should thus stand—and as it is printed here—neither "by" nor "be" is entirely acceptable with Chaucer's doublet, and the modern reader, like the medieval scribe, is left wondering which word Chaucer intended.

In addition to utilizing the Latin and French in order to present the semantic range he desires, Chaucer frequently creates doublets involving a derivative of one of his source words and a translation of the other. In the cases where there does not seem to be much semantic distinction between the two words, one is perhaps justified again in assuming that Chaucer's primary interest was simply the variations of expression in Latin, French and English. For example:

uestigia (1p3.24)	traces (24)	traces or steppes (45)
auctori (1p6.43)	feseur (47)	the auctour and the makere (82)
tua iura (3m5.6)	a tes commandemens (3-4)	at thy comaundementz or at thi lawes (5-6)
confiteri (3p10.56)	ottroier (59)	granten and confessen (108)

Where there is a semantic difference between the French and Latin, this difference falls into the expected patterns, so that one of Chaucer's words expresses the literal meaning of the Latin, for instance, while the other reflects the figurative meaning of the French:

neglectae (1p1.15)	despite (14)	forleten and despised (25-26)
compta (1m5.38)	couvers (26)	covered and kembd (44)
nondum... transcenderat (2p7.27-28)	n'avoit onques trespassé (31-32)	ne hadde nat yit passid ne clomben (61-62)[18]

Where the French expresses the literal meaning of the Latin, Chaucer may pair it with a word suggesting the figurative meaning:

sic considera (2p7.8)	ainsi le pues veoir (9)	see now and considere (20-21)[19]

On one occasion Chaucer, by translating the Latin and creating a derivative of the French, duplicates Jean's mistranslation: "uelut insultans" (2p7.65), "aussi comme en soi esjoissant" (73-74) and "as in stryvynge ayen and rejoysynge of hymself" (134-35). Perhaps Jean read "exsultans" instead of "insultans," but why Chaucer should have followed this contextually inappropriate reading, when his manuscript clearly had "insultans," is unclear.

Chaucer also creates doublets formed of derivatives of both the Latin and the French. As with those that involve only one derivative, there seems to be no pattern to the order in which the words occur. Moreover, in most cases the doublets containing two derivatives seem to achieve no semantic distinction. Why this should be so is problematic. While Chaucer was not trying out new words — since the derivatives were by nature current in his day — he may simply have been attempting to use as many words as possible. Such doublets certainly constitute "literal" translations, and in a few instances alliteration might be the "raison d'être." For example:

affectuum (1p1.28)	entalentemenz (29)	talentz or affeccions (53-54)
fraudes (1p4.52)	tricheries (62)	trecheries and frawdes (118-19)

posse dissolui (3p8.27)	puet estre destruit (28)	mai ben destroied or dissolvid (53-54)
dispositio (4p6.29)	l'ordenance (35)	the disposicioun and ordenance (64-65)
compellit (5p4.45)	constraingne (53)	constreynith or compelleth (94)

The French derivative may represent the figurative meaning of the Latin, while the Latin derivative may suggest the literal meaning:

claris...honoribus (2m2.11)	noblez honneurs (7-8)	noble or cleer honours (12)
praeclara (2p5.91)	precieuse et noble (109)	precyous and ryght cleer (185-86)

The remainder of Chaucer's doublets falls into a variety of familiar types. If one French word is able to capture two meanings of one Latin word, Chaucer may use a doublet: "protexi" (1p4.33), "couvri" (34) and "have I covered and defended" (62). Chaucer may also expand on the implications of the Latin and French words. For instance, in the following examples the added words reflect Chaucer's interpretations of the semantic subtleties of the originals:

capessendae (1p4.18)	d'enprendre (19)	to taken and desire (34-35)
Ne...corriperet (1p4.43-44)	ne surprist (52-53)	ne schulde nought sodeynli henten ne punysshe wrongfully (99-101)
comptos (1p5.18)	aournees (22)	apparayled and wrought (40)
premunt (2p7.15)	contiennent (18)	contene and overgoon (36-37)

Similarly, Chaucer's doublets may express the benefits or condition which result from what the Latin and French nouns signify:

studium (1p4.113)	l'estude (130)	studie and bountes (244)

45

ualentiam (3p2.34)   puissance (34)   power and worthynesse
                                                (63)

The adoption of source words in his translation is the final technique Chaucer uses in his lexical selection. There are two types of adoption: the use of a native word which is a derivative of the word it is translating, and the use of a source word not previously recorded in English. Although derivatives have been incidentally noted throughout the previous discussion, more detailed consideration will be given to them here. Generally, the morphology of Chaucer's derivatives matches that of their sources as much as possible, but Chaucer never imitates the affixes of his source words if these affixes are not also functional aspects of Middle English word formation. For example: "disposite" (4p6.140), "ordeneement" (158) and "ordeynly" (283), where Chaucer substitutes the Middle English adverbial suffix "-ly" for the Old French "-ment."[20]

Geissman (1952:37), in his discussion of Chaucer's translations from the French, suggests that the usage of derivatives "is so pronounced, especially in the prose translations, that one can only conclude that it is a deliberate technique, one further device for making the translations as literal as possible." But entirely "literal" translation, as is clear from Jean's and Chaucer's treatments of Latin idioms, is often meaningless. In his translations Chaucer evidently desired clarity and correctness, as Geissman (1952:143) points out, and does not seem intentionally to have sacrificed them merely for literalness. Derivatives are certainly literal translations, but since most of Chaucer's derivatives in *Boece* are of abstract or philosophical nouns, and since by the late fourteenth century most of the abstract and philosophical nouns in English were of romance origin, derivatives frequently were Chaucer's most logical choices. Of course, he could have used native words or other romance words, but why should he have passed up the convenience derivatives so obviously afforded him?[21] Moreover, the tradition of the wordlists—e.g. "to cownseyle" for "concilio"—suggests that derivatives were acceptable medieval English translations, although not at all as pervasive as they are in *Boece*.

For the most part, when Jean employs derivatives of philosophical and abstract words—generally nouns—Chaucer does so, too. For example:

ignorantia (3m8.2)	ignorance (1)	ignorance (1)
infirmitas (4p2.67)	enfermeté (68)	infirmite (136)
participatione (4p4.52)	participacion (59)	participacioun (114)
accusationis (4p4.123)	accusacion (142)	accusacioun (273)
praedestinatione (4p6.11)	predestinacion (14)	predestinacioun (28)
temporalis ordinis (4p6.33-34)	ordenance temporelle (40)	temporel ordenaunce (73-74)
possessione (5p2.18)	possession (20)	possessioun (34)
imaginatio (5p4.73)	ymaginacion (85)	ymaginacioun (155)
intellegentia (5p4.74)	intelligence (85-86)	intelligence (156)
condicionem (5p6.80)	condicion (91)	condicioun (154)

Jean's occasional use of derivatives for verbs and adjectives also influences Chaucer's lexical selection:

perdurat (3p5.2-3)	dure (2)	dureth (3)
coniuncta (3p10.100-101)	fust conjointe (111)	were conjoyned (203)
recordor (4p2.28)	recorde (29)	recordeth (54)
remordet (4p6.132-33)	remort (147)	remordith (265)
aspera (4p7.47)	aspre (51)	aspre (104)

As with all of the techniques of lexical selection discussed heretofore, Chaucer's understanding of the use and value of derivatives is illustrated by his independent use of them. That is, he creates derivatives on the French or Latin alone. Philosophical and abstract words, again, predominate:

perennem (2m4.1)	pardurable (1)	perdurable (2)
molestia (3p9.47)	tristece (54)	moleste (103)

More complex than simple derivatives are those which involve the alteration of the source word to a different part of speech and the use of this word in a periphrastic construction, some examples of which were included in the discussion of periphrasis in general. Even if the value of such alterations is not always clear, they do reveal a translator's sensitivity to meaning and grammatical structure. On occasion Jean's alterations may be the inspiration for Chaucer's:

| Similiter ratiocinari ...licet (3p9.54-55) | Et aussi poons nous faire semblablez raisons (60-61) | And ryght thus mai I make semblable resouns (114-15) |

This alteration of a Latin verb into another verb and a noun derived from the Latin verb is the most common type of periphrastic derivative in both Jean's and Chaucer's translations. Chaucer, however, uses this technique much more frequently than Jean and creates other types of periphrastic derivatives as well. Since the lexicons of Latin and French are more similar than those of Latin and English, it is true that Jean needed to create fewer periphrastic derivatives than Chaucer did. Still, Chaucer's use of the technique is another demonstration of his competence as philologist and translator. Some examples of the alteration of a verb, Latin or French, into a noun and verb are:

si...conferatur (2p7.11)	se elle estoit comparee (12)	yif ther were maked comparysoun (27)
carent (3p3.12)	defaillent (13)	there be defaute (19-20)
"Nec ambigo," inquam, "quin... satisfacerem" (4p4.109)	"Je ne doute pas," dis je, "que je ne feisse suffisant amende" (126-27)	"I ne doute nat," quod I, "that I nolde doon suffisaunt satisfaccioun" (239-40)

In the last example, of course, although Jean creates the periphrasis of "satisfacerem," Chaucer contributes the derivative. Similar techniques are the alterations of a verb to another verb and either an adjective derived from the source verb or a noun, in a prepositional phrase, derived from it:

| discordant (2p7.34) | se descordent entreuz (38) | ben discordaunt (72-73) |
| simulauit (3p5.15) | fainst et monstra (15-16) | shewede by symylitude (25) |

Chaucer also employs a variety of other periphrastic derivatives, such as altering an adverb into a noun used adverbially, an adjective into a noun, and an adjective and noun into a noun and prepositional phrase:

Contraque (3p10.109)	Et encontre ce (120)	And the contrarie (220-21)
consequens est (4p3.40-41)	par quoy il s'ensuit (42)	than is this the consequence (82)
inter illas abundantissimas opes (3p3.15)	entre ces tres habondans richecez (16)	in the habowndaunce of alle thilke rychesses (25-26)[22]

Chaucer may also blend the Latin and French by taking a derivative from one language but altering it to the part of speech found in the other:

| Dissonare...uidentur (5p4.58) | il i semble avoir descort (67-68) | thei semen to discorden (122) |

Derivatives, simple and periphrastic, are conveniences, and as such they can occasionally cause problems of interpretation. The simplest problems result from using a word in an unusual, but not unattested, sense:

| tanti criminis fidem (1p4.128-29) | fai et creance de si grant blasme (145) | feith of so greet blame (274) |

Latin "fidem" here should be translated as "confirmation," and although this meaning is not recorded for "faith," a related meaning — "credence given to an opinion" — is [*MED*, s. v. sense 3.(b)]. Indeed, Chaucer himself uses "faith" in this sense: "And to hem yive I feyth and ful credence" (*LGW* f.31). Such problems are the simplest, because they arise only for the twentieth-century reader and not, one presumes, for the fourteenth-century one. Even the fourteenth-century reader, however, would occasionally have been misled by Chaucer's derivatives. For example:

| maleficio (1p4.129) | malefice (146) | malefice or enchauntement (275-76) |

This is the first time "malefice" is recorded in English, but from the fourteenth through the nineteenth century it is generally

49

used in the sense "sorcery"; the sense "wickedness" is not recorded until late in the sixteenth century. The only other time Chaucer uses "malefice" — at *CT*.X.341 — it is in the phrase "by malefice of sorcerie," and the *Medulla* (366) translates "maleficium" as "wychcrafte." Thus, it is reasonable to conclude, given the history of "malefice" and the fact that Chaucer here pairs it with "enchauntement," that Chaucer misread the Latin and French, which mean only "misdeed," and intended the derivative in the sense "sorcery." One final problem which can arise from derivatives has been pointed out, in a different context, by Olga Fischer (1979:633): "Chaucer does not really distinguish between the different senses a word can have in either Latin or French." Although perhaps overstated, the issue is an important one. If the English derivative Chaucer employs does not have the semantic range of the source word, the English translation is necessarily not as semantically precise as the original. By way of example Fischer notes that Chaucer almost invariably translates Latin "fortuna" with "fortune," even though the Latin word is used in senses as disparate as "fate" and "prosperity."[23]

The other words which Chaucer adopts from his sources are derivatives which are also neologisms — words not previously recorded in English. Although there are neologisms from Germanic roots — such as "skillynge" (4p6.140) and "forwytere" (5p6.295) — the vast majority are of romance origin. The use of neologisms certainly suggest an author's lexical creativity and ingenuity, but the various problems involved with the determination of them must temper the use of them as evidence in any argument. First, given the inadequate resources available, one can never be sure if the earliest citation in the *OED* or *MED* is in fact the first time a word was used. Probably more medieval literature has been lost than has survived, and, as notes in philological journals demonstrate every year, lexicographers do not always find the earliest occurrence in the works which have survived. Moreover, the dating of many medieval texts is uncertain. Indeed, few of Chaucer's works can be precisely dated — did Chaucer write the *House of Fame* before or after *Boece*? — so even if Chaucer seems to be the first to use a given word, one cannot be sure where he used it first. A second problem with the determination of neologisms is grammatical. If a present participle is first recorded in 1400, but the finite verb form is recorded in 1350, should the present participle be regarded as a neologism? Even if the present participle is being used substantively, does not the finite verb presuppose its existence? Most lexicographers would answer "no" and credit the author who used the present participle with a neologism. Yet this procedure is perhaps more of a lexicographical convenience than an insight into the psychology of word formation. Finally, with respect to what neologisms can reveal about Chaucer's creativity, Chaucer, unlike more recent writers, almost certainly was unaware that he was creating neologisms. A Lewis Carrol can create "mimsy" and "gimble" knowing full well he is inventing new words, but such intentional neologisms are rather alien to medieval notions of language; they first appear in abundance in the so-called "inkhorn terms" of the sixteenth century. Moreover, Chaucer might have thought "skillynge," for instance, was an unusual word, but since he obviously did not have an *OED* or *MED*, he could not have known that he was the first—and would be the only—writer to use it.[24] Chaucer clearly did know, indeed, that some of his "neologisms" were unusual words, for he occasionally glosses them or pairs them with more common words of the same meaning. Nevertheless, the evidence of the neologisms should not figure too prominently in an assessment of Chaucer's lexical creativity in *Boece*.

With these reservations, then, it will be appropriate to offer a brief classification of the neologisms in *Boece*. They represent every part of speech, but they can be divided into two major types: abstract or philosophical words and concrete words. The former type is necessitated, of course, by the complexity of the ideas of the *Consolation* in relation to the available English vocabulary.[25] For example:

compensatione (4p4.126)	recompensacion (145)	recompensacioun (280)
imaginaria (5p4.101)	ymaginative (118)	ymaginatyf (211)
praesentarium (5p6.37)	presentaire (39)	presentarie (69)

TECHNIQUES OF TRANSLATION

Some examples of verbs, adjectives and concrete nouns which are neologisms are:

uererer (1p3.12)	redouteroie (12)	redowte (19-20)
praeiudicatae (1p4.43)	devant juigee (52)	ajugid byforn (99)
rapientes (1p3.41)	ravisseurs (42)	ravyneres and henteres (80-81)

In the last example, "henteres" is the neologism.

In form, Chaucer's neologisms may be identical to their sources or contain small changes in accordance with English morphology:

imbriferos (3m1.8)	plungeux (6)[26]	plowngy (8)
coniunctione (3p11.32)	conjonction (32)	conjunccion (64)
refectus (4p6.187)	refaiz (206)	reffressched and refect (374)[27]

As the last example indicates, Chaucer may define his neologisms by doubling them with more common words (see Machan, 1984). On other occasions, he indicates the meaning of the new word by means of a lexical gloss. For example:

> conditori...coaeternum (5p6.30-31)
> ensemble pardurable avec son feseur (33-34)
> coeterne with his makere. (As who seith, thei wene that this world and God ben makid togidre eterne) (56-58)

The context of some of Chaucer's neologisms, such as "devysioun" in the following, makes their meanings clear:

> Quod enim simplex est indiuisumque natura (3p9.9)
> Car la chose qui est une et simple ne ne puet estre devisee (11-12)
> For thilke thyng that simply is o thing withouten ony devysioun (17-18)

The majority of Chaucer's neologisms, however, are unexplained, and their meanings would be clear only to someone who knew Latin or French:

proscriptioni (1p4.114)	essil (130)	proscripcion (243)
ineuitabili (5p1.50)	qui n'est pas eschevable (52)	uneschuable (95)
supplicandi (5p3.97)	supplicacion (108)	supplicacion (200-201)

Although the meaning of "uneschuable" might seem transparent enough, it would not be so to any fourteenth-century reader who did know French. The antonym "eschuable" is not recorded in either the *OED* or the *MED*; the common adjectival form in the fourteenth century was "eschue." The meaning of some of the neologisms Chaucer creates from Germanic roots can also be ambiguous. For example, Chaucer translates "ratiocinatio" (4p6.69) and "parole" (78) with "skillynge" (140). This is the only time the deverbal noun "skillynge" is recorded in the *OED*. Although Chaucer himself uses the noun "skill" in the sense "reason," the verb "skillen" is never recorded in the sense "to reason"; the most approximate sense is "to understand, comprehend" (*OED*, s. v. "skill" v. sense 4.a), first recorded in 1500. Thus, "skillynge" is a deverbal noun with a denominal meaning — a rather odd combination at best.[28]

As was stated at the beginning of this chapter, a translator's primary problem is to match the words of his original with words in his own language which have similar semantic ranges and connotations, and the success or failure of his translation depends on how well he solves the lexical problems he faces. By viewing Chaucer's translation in its fourteenth-century milieu, one sees that *Boece*, on this primary level, must be regarded as a successful translation. Most of the native words Chaucer employs are used in perfectly acceptable fourteenth-century senses, and the largely "Latinate" vocabulary of *Boece* is necessitated by the number of philosophical and abstract words in the *Consolation* and Jean's translation. Moreover, some of the verbosity of *Boece* was all but required by the linguistic resources Chaucer had; if English lacked a one-word equivalent of a given Latin or French word, Chaucer had to form a periphrasis. Had Chaucer lived 400 years earlier, he might have used "wyrtmyhtig" instead of "myghti over the erbes" for "herbipotens"; to fault him for not doing so is to make a rather pointless comparison between Old and Middle English. The difficulties Chaucer had in translating Latin idioms are also understandable within the linguisic milieu in which *Boece* was produced. All idioms present translation

53

problems—Jean de Meung had little more success with Latin idioms than Chaucer did—and the Latin-English wordlists suggest that the late Middle Ages did not have a translation tradition for them. That Chaucer should have followed the French in the translation of idioms, and the French and the wordlist tradition in other lexical problems, is simply a tribute to his good judgment.

The various lexical techniques Chaucer employs indicate that one of his primary concerns was the expression of the ideas of the *Consolation*. By expanding on the calques and periphrases suggested by Jean and the wordlist tradition, Chaucer reveals that he is not a slavish imitator but a word-loving innovator. The use of calques in medieval translation has not been discussed in detail, but a comparison between Chaucer's and Richard Rolle's calques certainly favors Chaucer.[29] Similarly, Chaucer surpasses his contemporaries in the effective use of doublets. Although doublets in medieval translation are generally regarded as tautological or simply stylistic, Lawler (1983:279) has suggested that in many of the ones Trevisa uses in his translation of *De Proprietatibus Rerum* "the first member is derived from Latin, usually Bartholomaeus's actual word, the second a native English synonym." Lawler feels that such doublets reveal Trevisa's awareness of the problems of meaning and of the needs of his audience: "In many cases Trevisa must have felt the latinate word more exact and yet only half-naturalized, unfamiliar to his readers, and so in need of glossing." Yet this is scarcely as sophisticated a use of doublets as Chaucer's combinations of literal and figurative and literal and extrapolated meanings. This use of doublets, suggested by Jean but developed by Chaucer, demonstrates greater awareness of semantic range and greater competence in translation. This semantic awareness and translation competence is also evident in many of Chaucer's combined translations; if both the Latin and the French expressed meanings which Chaucer thought were pertinent, he simply, yet skillfully, used both.

If one grants that Chaucer's vocabulary in *Boece* is effective and has a broad range, one needs still to consider its implications—Chaucer's purpose in using the lexicon he did. Early in this chapter it was suggested that if all of his translation techniques combine in a coherent pattern, one is justified in inferring the end to which these techniques were directed. The preceding discussion indicates that one end was the correct expression of the ideas of the *Consolation*. Throughout this chapter, however, another end has occasionally been mentioned: the simple manipulation of language. Indeed, this philologist's joy in experimenting with words and their structures is evident in several of Chaucer's techniques of lexical selection. His frequent use of calques, for instance, implies a sensitivity to word morphology.

Moreover, many of the native words Chaucer uses, such as "unwar" and "university," are used in senses not previously recorded. A glance through the *OED* and *MED* turns up many more examples of such "semantic extension," as it might be called. In part, of course, this may be attributed to our insufficient knowledge of the dates of fourteenth-century texts. Yet such words are so common in *Boece* that it seems reasonable to conclude that they constitute a conscious technique on Chaucer's part. Similarly, the derivatives and "neologisms" suggest that Chaucer was attempting to utilize all the available words. In short, that he intentionally used—and experimented with—an unnecessarily large vocabulary. Stewart (1891:221) was the first to suggest that Chaucer may have been trying out new words, but Jefferson (1917:26) contends that

> it hardly seems that Chaucer was seriously experimenting with new words for their own sake. In the first place he makes very little use of these words in his subsequent writings, as we might expect if he were interested in the words for themselves. In the second place his use of them sometimes indicates a carelessness which is hardly consistent with experimentation.

In support of the latter point, Jefferson (1917:27) cites the three different words Chaucer uses to translate Latin "fortuitus"—"fortunous," "fortuit" and "fortunel."[30] Yet both of Jefferson's arguments can be used against him. That Chaucer "made very little use of these new words in his subsequent writings" may simply indicate that, like many inventors, he was dissatisfied with some of his creations; and the "carelessness" of the three translations of "fortuitus" need not be carelessness at all but further evidence of Chaucer's experimentation with a variety of words. As Elliott (1974:160-61) suggests,

> that Chaucer was experimenting with words seems incontrovertible if we consider the types and morphemic structures involved, the use of certain words for rhetorical or rhythmic effect, alliteration, for example, as well as for the immediate contextual meaning required, and perhaps most significant, the valuable practice *Boece* afforded for further lexical inventiveness in *Troilus and Criseyde* and *The Canterbury Tales*.

Further evidence that Chaucer was experimenting with words is offered by the nonce words—words Chaucer uses only in *Boece*. Whereas Chaucer very likely could not know he was creating a neologism, he would be aware that a given word was rare—if not otherwise unattested—in his working vocabulary. Thus, nonce words, more so than neologisms, can be regarded as evidence of the creativity and experimentation in Chaucer's lexical selection. Elliott (1974:160) estimates that there are 150 nonce words in *Boece* but notes that "this may well be a very conservative estimate." Indeed, there are 517 nonce words.[31] By itself, this figure reveals nothing, but when *Boece* is compared with Chaucer's other prose translations, as in the following table, the figure speaks quite eloquently:[32]

	Astr	Mel	ParsT	Bo
pp. in Rob. edition	18	21	36	64
nonce words	85	95	205	517
nonce words per page	4.7	4.5	6.3	8.0
romance neologisms	53	23	53	247
percentage of lexicon which is romance neologisms	13.2	3.6	4.6	18.5

Compared with other prose works, then, *Boece* has much higher frequencies of nonce words and neologisms. A clear indication that Chaucer is trying out as many different words as possible is the fact that of the 517 nonce words, 346 are used only once. That at least 18.5% of its vocabulary consists of neologisms puts *Boece* highest in the Chaucerian canon in this category; the next highest, with 14.2%, is *To Rosemounde*. Although the philosophic content might partly explain why *Boece* has so many more nonce words and neologisms than the other translations, it cannot account for all such words.

Lexical experimentation also seems to underlie some of the structural manipulations Chaucer performs on words. Tautological doublets which consist of Latin adjectives and French prepositional phrases, or of simple and periphrastic superlatives, apparently exist only for the sake of the structural differences they embody. Since such doublets fit within the pattern of semantic and structural experimentation which is undeniable in Chaucer's other lexical techniques, it seems quite plausible that their structural differences are in fact their "raison d'être." The periphrastic derivatives and the combined translations in which Chaucer alters the original parts of speech are further evidence of his fascination with the structure — and restructuring — of words. Indeed, translations such as "felenous cursydnesse" for "nefas" and "felonnie" are as notable for their philological ingenuity as for their semantic expression. The full implications of Chaucer's lexical experimentation are far-reaching and will be discussed in detail in Chapters Five and Six.

CHAPTER 3

SYNTAX

This tretis, divided in 5 parties, wol I shewe the under ful light reules and naked wordes in Englissh, for Latyn ne canst thou yit but small, my litel sone. But natheles suffise to the these trewe conclusions in Englissh as wel as sufficith to these noble clerkes Grekes these same conclusions in Grek; and to Arabiens in Arabik, and Jewes in Ebrew, and to the Latyn folk in Latin; whiche Latyn folk had hem first out of othere dyverse langages, and writen hem in her owne tunge, that is to seyn, in Latyn. And God woot that in alle these langages and in many moo han these conclusions ben suffisantly learned and taught, and yit by diverse reules; right as diverse pathes leden diverse folk the righte way to Rome. (*Pref. Astr.*25-40)

In the translation of individual words, a translator is primarily concerned with semantic problems; he must find words in his own language which match the words of his source in denotation and connotation. Although syntax also involves semantics—syntactic context and construction contribute much to a word's meaning—the problems syntax creates are primarily grammatical: a translator must not only naturalize the word order of his source but also translate constructions which may be outside of the formal possibilities of his own language. For instance, an English translator of Greek has to create a construction that can stand for the genitive absolute, which simply cannot be created in English. Indeed, an English translator of Greek or Latin faces particularly difficult syntactic problems, for the latter are synthetic languages, while English is analytic. Although fourteenth-century English bears more grammatical similarities to its synthetic ancestor Old English than Modern English does, Chaucer's language is nevertheless in large part analytic, too. Consequently, the syntactic problems Chaucer confronts in translating Latin into English could be as formidable as the semantic ones. The French of Jean de Meung presents considerably fewer syntactic problems, for structurally Old French stands, as it were, halfway between Latin and Middle English; it has a wider set of inflections than Middle English, but word order is more important in Old French than in Latin.

Chaucer's solutions to the syntactic problems he faces have generally been disparaged by critics. Krapp (1915:10), for instance, is rather blunt in his assessment:

> The main defects of the translation are crudity and awkwardness, even at times, obscurity, of expression, due to imperfect adaptation of the thought to the English idiom. Chaucer's difficulties arose from the embarrassment caused by the necessity of striking a balance between a Latin and an English phrasing.

Chute (1946:155) charges Chaucer's syntax with the same fault others have seen in his vocabulary — anxious literalness:

> Chaucer moved through the *Consolation of Philosophy* inch by inch, anxiously attempting to reproduce the original literally and exactly at all points, and produced a complex, Latinized English which is very unlike the clear, simple sentences that were in his normal element of poetry.

And Robinson (1957:320) suggests that "the use of a French translation, heavily glossed, alongside of the Latin original contributed to looseness of structure and diffuseness of language." But Chute's and Robinson's comments are contradictory. On the one hand, Chute accuses Chaucer of using "Latinized English," and on the other, Robinson accuses him of using "loose" and "diffuse" structures under the influence of the French. "Latinized English," since Latin is a synthetic language, is presumably compact and elliptical. But if Chaucer's syntax is compact, it cannot very well be diffuse as well.

The objective of this chapter, then, is to offer an account of Chaucer's syntax in *Boece*—to determine how effectively he responds to the grammatical problems and syntactic subtleties of Latin and French. To this end, the first part of the discussion will focus on certain grammatical shibboleths, so to speak, and Chaucer's treatment of them; the next part of the discussion will consider how Latin and French have influenced the syntax of *Boece*; and the last part will assess some of the techniques Chaucer uses to alter or clarify the syntax of his originals. Syntax is a broad topic, and the limitations of space preclude an exhaustive study of all of Chaucer's syntactic techniques. Here, the attempt is to analyze only Chaucer's major syntactic techniques, and while several minor constructions are passed over in silence, the examples offered herein are intended to characterize Chaucer's general approach to syntax in *Boece*.

Indeed, the syntactic techniques selected for discussion here suggest that, like his lexicon, Chaucer's syntax, when viewed in the proper linguistic milieu and in relation to the objectives of his translation, is clear and effective. The quotation from the *Astrolabe* which prefaces this chapter could be regarded as a fair description of Chaucer's syntax in *Boece* as well. For the most part, Chaucer uses "light reules"—simple grammatical constructions[1]—in such a way that the "trewe conclusions" of the *Consolatio* "suffise" in English as well as they do in Latin and French. It is not the English of Chaucer's original poetry, but then, quite obviously, *Boece* is not original poetry. Just as the lexicon of *Boece* is tailored to the end of the accurate expression of the ideas of the *Consolation*, so, too, is its syntax. Chaucer generally avoids constructions which are alien to English, and the foreign constructions which he does import are almost aways transparent. Chaucer's aim is clearly to stay as close as possible to the Latin and French while still composing intelligible English.

Different languages have different syntactic structures characteristic of them. For instance, Greek has genitive absolutes, Old Icelandic has genitives of respect, and Modern German has suspension of adverbs in separable verbs. These structures may appear in other languages as well, but the frequency of genitives of respect in Old Icelandic, for example, is one of the distinguishing characteristics of that language. Similarly, although impersonal verbs are used in Modern English, they occur much more frequently in Latin. Some structures, however, also prove to be what might be called grammatical shibboleths. That is, although a given construction may be created in a certain language, the construction is unidiomatic — if not ungrammatical — and thus serves to distinguish two languages in structure. For example, to return to the Old Icelandic genitive of respect, the beginning of *Eiríksmál* is "Hvat's þat drauma?" Literally, this means "What is that of dreams," which makes for unnatural — although intelligible — English, because the strict genitive of respect is alien to it. Rather, in idiomatic English the phrase would be "What kind of dream is that?"

Latin, in comparison with Middle English, has several such grammatical shibboleths: ablative absolutes, complex participles, and complex impersonal verbs without expressed subjects. Although all of these structures are used in Middle English, they are unidiomatic and marked, and indeed the first two originally appeared in English as imitations of the corresponding Latin structures. These first two structures in particular are singled out in the Purvey preface as those in need of transformation, for "if the lettre mai not be suid in translating, let the sentence euere be hool and open, for the wordis owen to serue to the entent and sentence, and ellis the wordis ben superflu either false" (Forshall and Madden, 1850:1.57). In many cases, the reason imitation of these structures is unidiomatic is that they are embedded in long and complex sentences which Middle English, with its predominance of paratactic clauses, cannot duplicate exactly. A good way of assessing the naturalness of Chaucer's syntax, then, is to examine his response to such structures. If he imitates ablative absolutes, for instance, his syntax may be called Latinate; if he employs a native English structure to stand for them, it may not be.

Jefferson (1917:39-41; also see Stewart, 1891:217-18) was one of the earliest critics to discuss Chaucer's expansions of Latin ablative absolutes and like syntactic forms, but it was Cline (1928:45) who first attempted to define what Chaucer was doing. Picking up on a phrase in the Purvey preface to the second Wycliffite Bible, he called the procedure "open translation" and noted that "it meant an *opening* of the close Latin absolute and participle constructions to English clauses." A brief passage from the Purvey preface, composed about 1395, is relevant here:

> In translating into English, manie resolucions moun make the sentence open, as an ablatif case absolute may be resoluid into these thre wordis, with conuenable verbe, *the while, for, if*, as gramariens seyn; as thus, *the maistir redinge, I stonde*, mai be resoluid thus, *while the maistir redith, I stonde*, either *if the maistir redith*, etc. either *for the maistir*, etc.; and sumtyme it wolde acorde wel with the sentence to be resoluid into *whanne*, either into *aftirward*, thus, *whanne the maistir red, I stood*, either *aftir the maistir red, I stood*; and sumtyme it mai wel be resoluid into a verbe of the same tens, as othere ben in the same resoun, and into this word *et*, that is, *and* in English, as thus, *arescentibus hominibus prae timore*, that is, *and men shulen wexe drie for drede*. (Forshall and Madden, 1850:1.57)

While open translation is a given in Modern English translations, it is clear from the Purvey preface that the technique was something of a novelty in the late fourteenth century, despite the repeated affirmations of Jerome's "sense for sense" dictum. In 1383 the first part of the first Wycliffite Bible lacks the technique, but the first revision, completed in 1384, does contain open translations. In 1387 Trevisa regularly employs open translation, and by the fifteenth century the technique is, with a few exceptions, quite common (see Workman, 1940). Chaucer and Jean employ open translation inconsistently, though the technique is more common in *Boece* than in *Li Livres*. Furthermore, Chaucer's use of open translation, as the end of this chapter will make clear, is decidedly different from Trevisa's and the Wycliffites' use. For the present, it will suffice to note that the inconsistency in Chaucer's use of the technique in about 1380 is due to the fact that open translation had not been universally adopted when he wrote. Moreover, Ellis (1982:34) points out that "a translator is unlikely to achieve absolute consistency of practice" but that his "practices have a cumulative and quantifiable effect." If the cumulation of Chaucer's practices in *Boece* is examined, it is clear that he preferred open translation to the imitation of primarily Latin structures.[2]

Why a technique as logical as open translation should not have been developed until relatively late in the Middle Ages is problematic. Perhaps the desire to preserve the original Latin texts or the respects given to Latin as a "better" language accounts for the late adoption of the technique. In the case of Scripture, there was almost certainly a reluctance to alter the word of God. Indeed, as Ellis (1982:30) points out, the eloquence of Purvey and Trevisa[3] in their descriptions of and explanations for open translation probably resulted from their awareness "of the need to defend themselves against the claim of the literalists that only those Bible translations could be permitted which exactly observed the grammatical forms of their original."

In any event, Chaucer clearly perceived the value of expanding ablative and participial constructions. Whether he decided to use expansions on his own or on the model of Jean's practice and suggestion in his preface — "que je preisse plainement la sentence de l'aucteur sens trop ensuivre les paroles du latin" (Dedeck-Héry, 1952:168) — is debatable. Cline (1928:73) notes that the "most immediate explanation of [Chaucer's expansions] is, of course, the French source; and the explanation of [the French expansions] is that they are quite in accord with the objects of 'open' translation." Indeed, many of Chaucer's expansions are indebted to the French, but when Jean does not expand an ablative absolute, Chaucer very frequently does, thus revealing that open translation was, like calques and periphrases, a functional aspect of his translation technique. In many cases, Jean's expansions include verbal additions which help to clarify the meaning of the terse Latin; Chaucer generally follows these additions. For example:

> principio cognito (1p6.25)
> puis que tu cognois le commencement des chosez (26-27)
> syn thow knowest the bygynnynge of thynges (47)

> me abeunte (2p2.17)
> quant je me depart (19)
> whan I wende (32)

> sed occupato ad imagines uisu (3p1.16-17)
> mais pour ce que ta veue est empechiee pour l'ymaginacion des chosez terriennes (20-21)
> but forasmoche as thi syghte is ocupyed and destourbed by imagynacioun of erthly thynges (36-38)

> Deficiente etenim uoluntate (4p2.13-14)
> Car se volenté fault (15)
> For yif that wille lakketh (26)

> Cur enim relicta uirtute uitia sectantur (4p2.82)
> Car pour quoy laissent il vertus et ensuivent les vices (85-86)[4]
> For whi forleten thei vertus and folwen vices (170-71)

> Quo semel recepto (5p3.77)
> Et se ce est foiz receu et ottroié (84)
> And yif this thing be oonys igrauntid and resceyved (150-51)

In these examples one sees Chaucer, following Jean, "resolving" the ablative absolutes with several of the words Purvey mentions: "when," "for" and "if." Moreover, all of Jean's additions are contextually appropriate responses to the brief Latin. The second to last example indicates one of the most common results of open translation, parataxis, which will be discussed later in this chapter.

When creating his own expansions of ablative absolutes, Chaucer utilizes the same techniques suggested by the Purvey preface and Jean's translation: conjunctions, contextually appropriate additions and parataxis.

abreptisque ab ea panniculis (1p3.22-23)
et les girons arrachiéz (22)
and with tho cloutes that thei hadden arased out of my clothes (41-42)

dimotis fallacium affectionum tenebris (1p6.53)
les tenebres des decevans desiriers ostees (57)
aftir that the derknesse of desceyvynge desyrynges is doon away (100-101)

et relicta conscientiae uirtutisque praestantia de alienis praemia sermunculis postualtis (2p7.57-58)
et, delaissiee de la grant valeur de conscience et de vertu, requeréz vos loiers de paroles estranges (63-64)
and ye forsaken the grete worthynesse of concience and of vertu, and ye seeken yowr gerdouns of the smale wordes of straunge folke (116-19)

Chaucer also expands other ablative constructions which are alien to English. In the following passage it is an ablative of respect which Chaucer opens up:

si grata intuitu species est (2p5.42)
se la biauté en est agreable par regart (52)
yif the beaute be aggreable to loken uppon (86-87)

Jefferson (1917:41) seems to regard Chaucer's expansions as aberrations which are probably stylistically motivated: "The reason for the various expansions to be found in the translation is not always apparent. Sometimes, however, they seem designed for rhetorical effect." The "rhetorical effect" which Jefferson perceives is the "metrical quality" of *Boece*. Similarly, Cline (1928:73), even though he recognizes the clarity Chaucer's expansions produce, suggests that where "neither the necessities of translation nor the French model accounts for [the expansions], one may assume that they involve some rhetorical principle." Both interpretations seem to put style before content. Moreover, they also suggest that the expansions which create natural English syntax in *Boece*, not the imitations of Latin constructions, are what must be justified. But surely just the opposite is true: If Chaucer was able to naturalize Latin syntax, how does one account for the passages where he does not? The answer, as was suggested above, lies in the fact that open translation had only begun to be utilized when Chaucer wrote *Boece*; the technique would have been adopted — by individual translators as well as by translators in general — gradually and not immediately, just as, for instance, morphological and phonological changes, while they are taking place, are gradual, not discrete. Thus, Chaucer's inconsistent use of open translation is just what one would expect. Moreover, Chaucer's debt to the French must be taken into consideration, for in many cases where Chaucer has not naturalized Latin syntax, neither has Jean. This imitation recalls Chaucer's preservations of Jean's tautological doublets. Of course, this explanation does not absolve Chaucer of the charge of bad judgment — and in most cases Chaucer's imitations of Latin constructions are awkward or ambiguous — but it does preclude placing all the responsibility with him. Some examples of Chaucer's and Jean's imitations of ablative absolutes are:

> tristitiae nebulis dissolutis (1p3.1)
> les nubleces de tristece dissolues (1)
> the cloudes of sorwe dissolved and doon awey (1-2)
>
> obiecta periculis auctoritate (1p4.32-33)
> par l'auctorité de moy contremise aus perilz (34-35)
> by the auctorite of me put ayens perils (that is to seyn, put myn auctorite in peril for) (62-64)
>
> luce reperta (3m9.23)
> ycelle clarté trouvee (25)
> the lyght ifounde (41-42)
>
> Quae si recepta futurorum necessitate nihil uirium habere credantur (5p3.97-98)
> Et se on croit que esperence ne prieres n'ont nulles forcez par la neccessité des chosez a avenir receue (109-10)
> And yif men ne wene nat that hope ne preieres ne han no strengthis by the necessite of thingis to comen iresceyved (203-206)

Chaucer may be praised for glossing the absolute construction in the second passage, but his decision to follow Jean's imitation in the last example is worse than bad. This occasional poor judgment is also evident when Chaucer imitates Latin ablative constructions, even though Jean has expanded them. For example:

> eodemque superstite (1p3.16-17)
> Et puis que Platon fu remés vis (16-17)
> And eek, the same Plato lyvynge (26-27)

The Purvey preface describes the expansion of participles, another aspect of open translation, as follows:

> Also a participle of a present tens, either preterit, of actif vois, eithir passif, mai be resoluid into a verbe of the same tens, and a coniunccioun copulatif, as thus, *dicens*, that is, *seiynge*, mai be resoluid thus, *and seith*, eithir *that seith*; and this wole, in manie placis, make the sentence open, where to Englisshe it aftir the word, wolde be derk and douteful (Forshall and Madden, 1850:1.57).

As is to be expected, given the gradual adoption of open translation, in their treatment of participles, as in their treatment of ablative absolutes, Jean and Chaucer are inconsistent. But in *Boece* the cumulation of Chaucer's practices again suggests that Chaucer preferred opening the constructions to imitating them. The one example in the Purvey preface is ambiguous, for "dicens" may be either a substantival or an adjectival participle. In any event, substantival participles are alien to English, and many of the participles which Chaucer (and Jean) expands are in fact substantival:

> hiantium (1p4.42)
> de ceus qui les ouvroient (51-52)
> of hem that gapeden (97-98)

> Fugiens (2m4.13)
> Ainsi se tu veulz foir (6-7)
> And forthi, yif thou wolt fleen (10-11)

> interius autem recepta (3p1.12)
> mais quant elles sont receues dedens (16-17)
> but whan they ben resceyved withynne a wyght (28-29)

Jean and Chaucer necessarily expand future participles, both active and passive, since neither French nor English have one-word equivalents of this Latin structure. Such participles are translated either by complete clauses or by infinitive phrases. For example:

Inuocandum... rerum omnium patrem censeo (3p9.89-90)[5]
je juge que nous devons apeler le pere de toutez chosez (99)
Y deme that we schul clepe to the Fadir of alle goodes (197-98)

nunc demonstrandum reor (3p10.2)
or croi je qu'il seroit bon a demonstrer (2-3)
now trowe I that it were good to schewe (4)

se adepturos putant (4p2.127)
il cuident aconsuivre (137)
thei wenen to ateynen (265)

Generally, when Jean imitates the various Latin participial constructions, Chaucer still expands them. Some examples of Chaucer's expansions of substantival participles are:

tibi obsequentes (1p4.14)
a toy obeissans (14-15)
to whom I have ben obeisaunt (25)

quaesita (2m2.13)
les chosez aquises (9)
that they han geten (14-15)

Chaucer also expands several other types of complex Latin participial constructions which Jean imitates. Although these expansions do occasionally make *Boece* "diffuse," they almost always result in more idiomatic English. For instance, participles used as verbal adjectives—e.g., "carrying" in "the boy, carrying his helmet, went to the game"—are restricted in Middle and Modern English. In Old English they might be expressed by compound participles (e.g., "helmberend," which actually is a noun) but such constructions were out of currency by the fourteenth century. Moreover, the structural complexities of verbal adjectives should be considered; to use the transformationalists' terms, they consist of a complete clause at the deep structure level which first is transformed into a relative clause and then appears in the surface structure with the deletion of the relative pronoun and copulative verb. Chaucer, of course, knew nothing of transformational grammar, but by the way he naturalizes verbal adjectives—by turning them into complete clauses—one must conclude that he did perceive their structural complexity.

Verbal adjectives, to be sure, are common in Old French, and Chaucer himself uses them in his poetry.[6] But given his objectives of clarity and correctness, Chaucer evidently was reluctant to imitate such participial structures in *Boece*, particularly so if they occur appositively in long and complex sentences. For example:

>fortunae in nos saeuientis (1p4.6)
>de fortune forsenant encontre nous (7-8)
>of Fortune, that waxeth wood ayens me (11-12)

>Conigastum...impetum facientem (1p4.28-29)
>Congaste fesant assaut (31)
>Conigaste, that made alwey assawtes (56-57)

Chaucer, unlike Jean, also regularly expands simple adjectival participles. Like verbal adjectives, adjectival participles can be perceived as being structurally complex—they, too, are full clauses in the deep structure but appear at the surface structure with the deletion of the relative pronoun and copulative verb. In the first example given below, "tremendos" and "redoutables" are of course adjectives, not participles; yet the connection between "tremendos" and "tremere" is transparent, and Chaucer the philologist evidently saw the verb behind the adjective, so to speak.

>dudum tremendos...reges (2m1.3)
>les rois redoutables jadis (4)
>kynges that whilom weren ydradd (7-8)

>adeptis honoribus (3p2.16)
>par honneurs aquisez (18)
>by the honours that thei han igeten (32)

>acceptas escas (3p11.78)
>les viandez receues (83)
>the mete that we resseyven (156)

On occasion, Chaucer also employs open translation by expanding simple adjectives into clauses. Such expansions are difficult to explain, for he was unlikely to have interpreted a simple adjective and noun as being derived from the adjective, a copulative verb and the noun. For example:

SYNTAX

> saeuos tyrannos (1m4.11)
> les tyrans felons (8)
> tirauntz that ben wode and felenous (13-14)

When the adjective is postposed in the Latin, however, it is possible that Chaucer did perceive the adjective and noun as being derived from a full clause. For instance, in the following passage Chaucer may have understood the Latin and French to have a relative pronoun and the verb "est" in ellipsis:

> fortunae condicio cunctis mortalibus incerta (1p4.108)
> la condicion de fortune a touz mortiex hommes douteuse (124-25)
> condicion of fortune, that is uncerteyn to alle mortel folk (231-32)

It should also be noted that Chaucer frequently expands substantival adjectives, even though similar structures appear throughout his works:[7]

> iter innocentis (1p3.11)
> le chemin de li qui est innocent (11-12)[8]
> the weye of him that is innocent (18-19)

These unnecessary expansions of adjectives, which in part are influenced by the French, suggest a form of hyper-correction rooted in Chaucer's general preference for open translation.

In order to indicate the inconsistency in Jean's and Chaucer's techniques, included below are some examples of participles which Chaucer does not expand. Jean, again, has perhaps influenced some of Chaucer's syntactic imitations, as in the first passage:

> Et quid...tu...o omnium magistra uirtutum, a supero cardine delapsa uenisti (1p3.5-7)[9]
> O tu mestresse de toutez vertuz, descendue du souverain cardinal pour quoy es tu venue (5-6)
> O thou maystresse of alle vertues, descended from the sovereyne sete, why arttow comen (8-10)

> sed transuersos eos libido praecipitat (4p2.84-85)
> mais lecherie et couvoitise les en destourne et les trebuche (89)
> but lecherie and covetise overthroweth hem mystorned (176-77)

71

While the imitation of the Latin participial construction in the first passage makes for perfectly intelligible Middle English, the imitation in the second passage is indeed awkward. In general, there seems to be no pattern in the way Chaucer opens up a given Latin participial construction one time and imitates it the next, and this lack of a pattern is a good indicator of the ongoing adoption of open translation in the late fourteenth century.

The final grammatical shibboleth to be considered is the impersonal verb used without an express subject. Given the fact that so much of the *Consolatio* is logical argument, it is not surprising that this construction abounds in it. Impersonal verbs, with or without the expression of "it" as the undefined subject, are of course common in Middle English, though both structures gradually lost currency in the Middle Ages (see Mustanoja, 1960:131, 143 and 433-36, Visser, 1963: §3-50, and Burnley, 1983:35-37). But the *Consolatio* contains a number of complex structures involving an impersonal verb with unexpressed subject and a verbal complement. Both active and passive Latin verbs are involved, as well as phrases such as "necesse est." Though Chaucer in fact uses similar constructions in his poetry,[10] in most cases the Latin structure is so complex that an imitation of it in English would be extremely unidiomatic. Indeed, Chaucer, frequently influenced by the French, almost always translates with an active verb and an expressed subject. The passive construction is used quite often with an accusative-infinitive, as in the following example:

> Sed summum bonum beatitudinem esse concessum est (3p10.54-55)
> Mais nous avons ottroié que li souverains biens est beneurté (58)
> But we han graunted... that the sovereyn good is blisfulnesse (104-105)

Although Chaucer might have written something like "thynketh us sovereyn good to be blisfulnesse," the phrase is certainly Latinate and unidiomatic in Middle English. Chaucer, with or without the influence of the French, generally naturalizes impersonal active verbs when they are used in conjunction with an infinitive:

necesse est confiteri (3p9.34)
nous couvient il ottroier (41)
mote we graunten (78)

concludere licet (3p10.122-23)
poons nous... conclurre (135)
mowen we concluden (248)

A similar construction consists of an impersonal active verb and a finite verb. Whereas Jean regularly imitates the construction, Chaucer almost always naturalizes it. For example:

metuat necesse est (2p4.76-77)
il convient que il ait paour (88-89)
he mot alwey ben adrad (156)

Oportet igitur... concedas (3p11.21-22)
Donques couvient il que tu ottroies (22)
Thanne mustow graunten (44)

agnoscas licebit (4p2.4-5)
couviendra que tu cognoissez (5)
thow most nedes knowen (7)

oportet... differas (4p6.16)
il couvient que tu te seuffrez (19)
thou most suffren and forberen (37)

Chaucer's decision to naturalize these structures was a good one, for, again, while a translation such as "nedeth hym that he mot ben adrad" is certainly intelligible, it is not at all as natural for Middle English as is Chaucer's construction involving "mot." On the other hand, it should be noted that some other impersonal constructions—involving adjectives or simple finite verbs—can be imitated in Middle English without sounding particularly Latinate. For such constructions, Chaucer may or may not follow Jean's varying treatment. For example:

manifestum est (3p10.63)
C'est tout apert (67)
men mai seen (121-22)

manifestum est (3p10.74)
aperte chose est (79)
is it manifest and open (140-41)

apparet (3p10.119)
il apert (131)
it sheweth (240-41)

liquet (4p4.105)
nous sommes certain (121)
I am certein (228)

Chaucer's general avoidance, then, of ablative absolutes, complex participles and imperfect verbs without expressed subjects indicates a desire to remain as close as possible to his sources without producing unidiomatic or unnatural syntax. But when faced with a syntactic structure which was also current in Middle English, Chaucer frequently incorporates the structure in his translation. Such structures may be marked, but they are common enough outside *Boece* to permit one to assume that Chaucer's contemporaries would have considered them unexceptionable and would have had little trouble interpreting them. Although some of the structures occur as early as the Old English period, it is reasonable to conclude that Chaucer's use of them in particular passages was inspired by their occurrence in the Latin or French; in short, that Chaucer uses syntactic derivatives just as he uses lexical derivatives.

Chaucer employs two major syntactic derivatives from the Latin: the placement of the object first, and the accusative-infinitive construction. With regard to the first structure, which is common in both Latin and Old French, Jefferson (1917:32) notes:

> A common occurrence throughout the translation is that of a noun introducing a clause and standing without close grammatical connections with the clause. This characteristic may sometimes be explained as a device for gaining emphasis and sometimes as a result of Chaucer's having followed the Latin word-order very closely. The noun, for example, may stand in the Latin in the accusative case at the beginning of the sentence. Chaucer translates as if it were nominative, and then passing on discovers his mistake, but turns the sentence to suit his convenience without regard to sentence structure.

Some examples of these "detached nouns," as Jefferson calls them, are:

> Quae tamen ille... prouidentiae cernit intuitus (5p2.23-24)
> Et toutevois ces chosez voit cil regars de la divine pourveance (26-27)
>
> The whiche thingis natheles the lokynge of the devyne purveaunce seth (43-45)
>
> Hanc enim necessitatem non propria facit natura sed condicionis adiectio (5p6.96-97)
>
> Car ceste necessité condicionnelle sa propre nature ne la fait pas, ainçois la fait li ajustemens de la condicion (108-9)
>
> for certes this necessite condicionel — the propre nature of it ne maketh it nat, but the adjeccioun of the condicioun makith it (188-90)

Elliott (1974:156), referring to another passage, observes, "Sometimes the Latin word-order which permits the object to precede the subject leads Chaucer into slavish imitation, and the English rendering, when there is not artisitic justification for it, becomes unidiomatic, and jarring, particularly when influenced also by the French version." The passage which Elliott cites is indeed awkward, but it must be noted that the construction OSV was relatively common in Middle English[11] — even if it was a marked construction — and that Chaucer himself uses it elsewhere:

> The remenant of the tale if ye wol heere (*CT* III.981)
> A thousand Troyes whoso that me yave (*TC* 2.977)[12]

And the repetition of the object in the second example — "necessite" and "it" — is not out of the ordinary, for this structure is also common in Old, Middle and Early Modern English (see Visser, 1963: §598-603, and Roscow, 1981:73-75; cf. Mustanoja, 1960:133-34). Thus, even if some of Chaucer's constructions involving the object in the first position are awkward, one cannot call them "mistakes," as Jefferson does, and criticize him for them; he simply is using an accepted fourteenth-century syntactic structure.

The other syntactic derivative which Chaucer uses on the model of the Latin is the accusative-infinitive construction:

> ne te existimari miserum uelis (2p3.12-13)
> pour ce que tu ne vueillez cuidier que tu soies chetis (13-14)
> that thow schalt noght wilne to leten thiself a wrecche (25-26)
>
> Sed qui beati sint deos esse conuenit (4p3.24-25)
> Mais cil qui beneuréz sont, il couviant que il soient dieu (25-26)

> and thilke folk that ben blisful it accordeth and is covenable to ben goddes (48-49)

Accusative-infinitive constructions are certainly characteristic of Latin, yet they are also common throughout Middle English literature—with or without ellipsis of "to be," as in the first example (see Visser, 1963: §646-58, and Kerkhof, 1982: §179-83). In the second passage, Boethius omits a pronoun such as "eos," but the sentence still makes for perfectly acceptable Latin. Jean expands the accusative construction into a clause, but Chaucer imitates it. Although the lack of a pronoun referent for "goddes" may seem odd, similar constructions occur elsewhere in Chaucer's works, as in the following, where it is not expressed who is caused to "doon amys":

> Ire, siknesse, or constellacioun,
> Wyn, wo, or chaungynge of complexioun
> Causeth ful ofte to doon amys or speken.
> (*CT*.V.781-83)[13]

Chaucer's syntactic derivatives from the French, given the structural similarities between Old French and Middle English, are perhaps less noticeable than his derivatives from the Latin, but they are more pervasive. Indeed, it is the structural similarity between the two languages which allows readers to pass over the constructions without recognizing them as imitations of the French; otherwise, one might well call the syntax of *Boece* "Gallic" rather than "Latinate." As Eckhardt (1984:47) points out with respect to some of the very literal passages in the *Romaunt*, "That they can be at once so French and so English testifies to the closeness of the two languages at that time."[14] Thus, the many constructions involving a verb and a reflexive pronoun in *Boece* are entirely unexceptionable as Middle English, though in fact many of them are imitations of French structures. Another one of the most common syntactic derivatives from the French is the postposing of adjectives. For example:

> fatalis...necessitatis (4p6.181-82)
> neccessité destinable (200-201)
> necessite destinable (364-65)

> alternus amor (4m6.17)
> amour entrechanjable (10)
> Love entrechaungeable (19)

Postposed adjectives, of course, occur innumerable times in Chaucer's works, but plurally inflected adjectives are less common.[15] An example from *Boece* is:

> cunctorum ratione degentium (5p6.5-6)
> de toutez creaturez raisonnablez (6)
> of alle creatures resonables (9-10)[16]

Another very common and easily missed syntactic derivative from the French is the resumptive pronoun:

> An uos agrorum pulchritudo delectat (2p5.27-28)
> Et la biauté des chans ne vous delite elle pas moult (33-34)
> And the beaute of feeldes, deliteth it nat mochel unto yow (54-55)

Chaucer's "it" refers back to the subject, and, since the sentence is a question, by following the verb the pronoun makes the sentence more idiomatic. Resumptive pronouns are common in Old and Middle English (Visser, 1963: §67-75 and 598-600, and Roscow, 1981:66-72), but their frequency in *Boece* is certainly attributable to the influence of the French syntax. Also relevant here is the construction consisting of a noun with postposed and preposed adjectives. Although this construction dates back to the Old English period, in *Boece* it generally occurs as a syntactic derivative of the French construction:

> uera perfectaque bona (3p11.9)
> vrais biens ne parfaiz (9)
> verray goodis ne parfite (18)

As Elliott (1974:157) points out, this construction occurs numerous times in Chaucer's works; e.g., "But knowen for historial thyng notable" (*CT*.VI.156).[17]

Yet another common syntactic derivative from the French involves the use of a negative in a dependent clause, especially after the verb "douter":

> quod...lucebit ipso perspicacius Phoebo (3m11.7-8)
> Lors li aparra et luira, plus clerement que li soleus ne luist (5-6)

> And thanne thilke thing... schal lighte more clerly than Phebus hymself ne schyneth (9-12)

> "Mundum," inquit, "hunc deo regi paulo ante minime dubitandum putabas" (3p12.10-11)
> "Tu ne cuidoies pas," dist elle, "un pou ci devant que on deust doubter que cist mondez ne fust gouvernéz par dieu" (10-11)
> "Thou ne wendest nat," quod sche, "a litel herebyforn, that men schulde doute that this world nys governed by God" (22-24)

While this use of an expletive negative in dependent clauses is perhaps unusual in Middle English, the usage can be seen as an extension of the common Middle English technique of multiple negation (cf. Burnley, 1983:72).

One last syntactic derivative from the French is mentioned by Jefferson (1917:30-31) in a section entitled "Peculiarities in Sentence Structure" — the excessive use of "that." Chaucer does seem to use "that" with annoying frequency in *Boece*, but the restrictions of Middle English grammar and the influence of Jean's translation must be taken into consideration. In Middle English, "that" functioned as a relative and demonstrative pronoun, and as a conjunction, alone, doubled and in phrases. Given the fact that Chaucer was opening absolute and participial constructions into relative clauses, he was required to produce an abundance of "thats." Moreover, "that" was almost Chaucer's only choice in translating the French unstressed neuter demonstrative "ce" and the relative "que," which frequently occur together. For example:

> Sed dat cuique natura quod conuenit (3p11.53-54)
> Mais nature donne a chascune ce que il li couvient (55-56)
> For nature yeveth to everything that that is convenient (107-8)

> Quod uero quisque potest (4p2.20)
> Mais en ce que chascuns peut (21)
> And in that that every wyght may (40)

Before concluding this chapter, it will be appropriate to comment on a few miscellaneous aspects of Chaucer's syntax in *Boece*. Both Jefferson (1917:30) and Elliott (1974:156) mention Chaucer's excessive use of "and." As Jefferson suggests, on occasion "Chaucer's fondness for this conjuction plays havoc with the coherence of his sentences," but the use of "and" is not so much a choice of style among Chaucer and his contemporaries — as Jefferson implies — as a requirement of Middle English grammar. Paratactic constructions are far more prevalent than hypotactic constructions in Middle English, and the only coordinate conjunction available was "and."[18] It is unprofitable to fault Chaucer for not using more hypotactic constructions, when his language simply did not allow for them. Moreover, the "opening" of Latin substantival participles and verbal adjectives almost necessarily resulted in parataxis in both Middle English and Old French, where the construction was also quite common.

> extrema uero est seruitus cum uitiis deditae rationis propriae possessione ceciderunt (5p2.17-18)
> Mes la derreniere et la peeur servitude est quant elles sont abandonnees aus vicez et sont cheues de le possessione de leur propre raison (18-20)
> But the laste servage is whan that thei ben yeven to vices and han ifalle fro the possessioun of hir propre resoun (32-34)

> summamque tenet singula perdens (5m3.24)
> et retient la somme des chosez et pert les singularitéz (20-21)
> but it withholdeth the somme of thinges and lesith the singularites (45-47)

A subtle syntactic technique which Chaucer employs, often in conjunction with other syntactic changes, is the alteration or clarification of Latin and French clauses. For instance, in the following passage he makes the first clause concessive and substitutes a conditional clause for the second temporal clause in the Latin and French:

> Quae est igitur ista potentia, quam pertimescunt habentes, quam nec cum habere uelis tutus sis et cum deponere cupias uitare non possis (3p5.31-33)
> Quiex est donques ceste puissance que cil qui l'ont la redoubtent et craiment, et quant tu la voudras avoir tu ne seras pas asseur, et quant tu la desireras a laissier tu ne la pourras eschever (34-37)
> What thyng is thanne thilke poower, that though men han it, yet thei ben agast; and whanne thou woldest han it, thou n'art nat siker; and yif thou woldest forleeten it, thow mayst nat escheuen it (60-64)

TECHNIQUES OF TRANSLATION

Whether such alterations improve the logic of the sentence is perhaps a subjective judgment, but it can be argued that in this passage the concessive conjunction "though" helps to stress the idea that one actually has "power," while the conditional conjunction "yif" intensifies the opposition between one's wanting to relinquish "power" and one's inability to do so. In the following passage Chaucer alters a simple coordinate clause to a result clause:

> que cum altius caput extulisset ipsum etiam caelum penetrabat respicientiumque hominum frustrabatur intuitum (1p1.10-11)
> et quant elle levoit plus haut son chief, elle perçoit neis le ciel meismes et decevoit la veue des hommes regardans (9-11)
> and whan sche hef hir heved heyer, sche percede the selve hevene so that the sighte of men lokynge was in ydel (17-19)

The addition of "so that" clarifies the relationship between the acts described in the Latin and French: men's inability to see Lady Philosophy was a result of the fact that she had raised her head into the sky.

By the addition of various conjunctions and conjunctive adverbs, Chaucer also clarifies the logic of the Latin sentences without altering the relationships between individual clauses. In some cases, Chaucer's additions are indebted to the French. For example:

> Fortunae te regendum dedisti, dominae moribus oportet obtemperes (2p1.51-52)
> Tu as donné toi meismes a gouverner a Fortune; si convient que tu t'acordez aus meurs de ta dame (57-59)
> Thou has bytaken thiself to the governaunce of Fortune and forthi it byhoveth the to ben obeisaunt to the maneris of thi lady (108-11)

> Nunc desine amissas opes querere: quod pretiosissimum diuitiarum genus est, amicos inuenisti (2p8.20-22)[19]
> Or ne te complaing pas donques des richessez perdues ou ne les quiers plus, car tu as trouvé la plus precieuse maniere des richeces qui puisse estre trouvee, c'est a savoir vrais amis (25-28)
> Now pleyne the nat thanne of rychesse ylorn, syn thow hast fownden the moste precyous kynde of rychesses, that is to seyn, thy verray freendes (45-48)

SYNTAX

In the first example, the second clause clearly implies the result of the first, while in the second example, the second clause is causal. Jean's and Chaucer's addition of "si" and "forthi" in the first passage and "car" and "syn" in the second simply clarify these relationships.

For the most part, the conjunctions and transitions which Chaucer adds are his own, and these additions further reveal his concern with presenting the argument of the *Consolation* in a clear fashion. For instance, in the following passage, by adding "thanne," Chaucer again clarifies the implied relationship between the two statements:

> Atque utinam posset ulla! Respondissem (1p4.80-81)
> Certes je voudroie que aucune autre peust estre esperee! Je eusse respondu (94-95)
> Certes I wolde that som other fredom myghte ben hoped; I wold thanne han answeryd (179-81)

Chaucer also adds clarifying conjunctions at the conclusion of long, complex arguments, as in the following passage, where Lady Philosophy has just finished explaining the not self-evident proposition that good people are happy and bad people are miserable. Chaucer adds "thanne" in order to emphasize her conclusion.

> Et illa: "Bonos," inquit, "esse felices, malos uero miseros nonne concessimus" (4p4.44-46)
> Lors dist elle: "N'avons nous pas ottroié que li bons sont beneureus et que li mauvais sont chetis" (50-51)
> "Have we nat thanne graunted," quod sche, "that goode folk ben blisful and schrewes ben wrecches" (96-98)

A similar use of this technique is at the conclusion of a "prosa" or "metrum," where a conjunction or transition — "certes" in the following — can signal the end of the section:

> tamen atras pellere curas / miserasque fugare querelas / non posse potentia non est (3m5.8-10)
> toutevois se tu ne pues oster hors de toy tes mauvais desiriers et chacier hors de toy tes chetivez complaintez, ce n'est pas puissance (4-6)[20]
> yit yif thou maist nat putten awey thy foule dirke desires, and dryven out fro the wrecchide compleyntes, certes it nys no power that thow hast (8-11)

81

TECHNIQUES OF TRANSLATION

On occasion, Chaucer's conjunctions can be misleading, as in the following passage, where Chaucer's "Forwhy" introduces a causal clause whereas in the Latin and French the two clauses are simply in apposition:

> An hoc inter minima aestimandum putas quod amicorum tibi fidelium mentes haec aspera, haec horribilis fortuna detexit? Haec tibi certos sodalium uultus ambiguosque secreuit (2p8.16-19)
> Cuidez tu ore que tu doies tenir a petite chose ce que ceste fortune aspre et orrible qui t'a ci mis t'a descouvert les pensees de tes loyaus amis? Iceste a departi les visages certains et doubteus de tes compaignons (19-22)
> Wenestow than that thow augghtest to leeten this a litel thyng, that this aspre and horrible Fortune hath discovered to the the thoughtes of thi trewe freendes. Forwhy this ilke Fortune hath departed and uncovered to the bothe the certein visages and eek the doutous visages of thi felawes (32-39)

In general, however, the conjunctions and transitions which Chaucer adds are effective, and some of the most common of these additions are: "thus," "ryght so," "whan," "after that," "anon," "for," "but ayeinward," "whilom," "and yit" and "but natheles."

The syntax of *Boece*, then, is neither "Latinized" nor unnecessarily "diffuse." Working within the limitations of fourteenth-century English and towards the objective of a close but intelligible translation, Chaucer has effectively responded to the grammatical problems and syntactic subtleties of Latin and French. To be sure, he has produced some syntactic oddities, but for the most part, Chaucer has naturalized constructions such as ablative absolutes, which are alien to English grammar; he has used the convenience of syntactic derivatives, when a construction which occurred in his sources was also current in English; and he has occasionally clarified the syntactic relationships of his sources, particularly the Latin, since its synthetic nature allowed for an economy of expression which the analytic Middle English language could not imitate. In short, Chaucer has used a philologist's knowledge of the complete syntactic resources of his own language in order to translate the syntactic structures of his sources. He was not writing original poetry, and so he should not be expected to have produced syntax like that found in the *Troilus*.

By way of a conclusion to this discussion of Chaucer's syntax, it will be useful to consider how *Boece* stands in relation to other late medieval translations. It should first be noted that the closeness of *Boece* to its sources harmonizes well with the overall effect of many subsequent English translations. Workman (1940:114) analyzes thirty-eight fifteenth-century translations from Latin and French and concludes that the "great majority... are characterized by a minimum of alterations. There are a few exceptions in all; and in many there are omissions. But the strongly prevailing procedure in these [translations] was to match the grammatical construction of every sentence-member taken from the source with a native English equivalent."[21] Moreover, Chaucer's expansions of various grammatical shibboleths, as was indicated at the beginning of this chapter, reflect the then developing preference for open translation. Sven Fristedt has analyzed the Wycliffite Bibles and Trevisa's *Polychronicon* in an admirably thorough fashion, and a comparison between his findings and Chaucer's techniques is relevant here. Ablative absolutes and accusative-infinitive constructions are expanded by both Trevisa and the translators of the second Wycliffite Bible; word order is completely naturalized in the second Wycliffite Bible and, to a lesser extent, in Trevisa's translation as well;[22] participles are expanded in the second Wycliffite Bible and generally in Trevisa's translation (Fristedt, 1969:xliv-xlv and 1973:13, 15-18 and 21-22).[23] Clearly, Trevisa and the translators of the second Wycliffite Bible had similar objectives: to offer their translations in completely normalized English. They naturalized not only the grammatical shibboleths but constructions such as accusative-infinitives and OSV word order as well. Chaucer, on the other hand, is more selective; he naturalizes only what needs to be naturalized and leaves the rest, a practice which certainly indicates a desire for a close but correct translation. Ellis (1982:31) suggests that a translator had at least three approaches open to him in his rendering of the original's grammatical relations: a literal one, of the sort favoured by Rolle; a slightly freer one, of the sort favoured by the second version of the Wycliffe Bible; and a still freer one, on the model of Trevisa's declared practice.

According to this classification, then, Chaucer's responses to the syntax of his sources place *Boece* between the literal approach of Rolle and the slightly freer one of the Wycliffites.

CHAPTER 4

STYLE

I take it to be self-evident that the style of a translated work, if not actually parasitic on that of its original, can hardly be understood except in relation to it; emerges as the consequence of the [structural, lexical and grammatical] choices [a translator makes]...; and becomes interesting in itself only in proportion as the translation, for whatever reason, is becoming an original work. Furthermore, style exists only in relation to the conflicting demands... of the original, the audience, the tradition, and the translator himself. (Ellis, 1982:34)

Chaucer's lexical and syntactic techniques in *Boece* are varied, sophisticated and well-suited to the variety of problems he confronted, and his sensitivity to the verbal and grammatical nuances of Latin, Old French and Middle English is apparent throughout his translation. Heretofore, for the most part, critics have not explored the lexical and syntactic choices made by Chaucer, but instead have focused on the larger question of Chaucer's performance as a "stylist" in *Boece*. Yet lexicon and syntax are the fundamental components of style. If an opinion is not based on close analysis of them it becomes either a general impression or, although it may point to some of a work's stylistic features, a restricted account of the style of that work. Moreover, in the case of *Boece*, as was mentioned in the first chapter, critics have tended to regard Chaucer's composition as if it were an original work rather than a translation. Critical judgments formed from this perspective may adequately explain isolated instances of the style of *Boece*, but they necessarily misrepresent the overall style, for they do not assess the style in relation to its components—lexicon and syntax—or to the nature of *Boece* itself.

Indeed, as Ellis insightfully points out in the passage which prefaces this chapter, the style of a translation can be understood only in relation to its original, its audience, and the tradition in which it is produced. If the style of a translation becomes interesting without reference to the original, it is because the translation is no longer regarded as a translation but as itself an original work. For example, when one discusses the style of *Troilus*, one refers only at the outset to the materials Chaucer has borrowed or not borrowed from *Il Filostrato*—e.g. the omission of Boccaccio's dedication to his lady—and focuses rather on the new materials and the formal artistic techniques Chaucer has used in creating his poem. This is the case because, although *Troilus* may be regarded as a type of translation, Chaucer has so drastically and effectively restructured *Il Filostrato* that his poem is considered an artistic achievement in its own right. Several of Chaucer's most successful compositions, such as the *Knight's Tale*, may be regarded similarly.

But, as the two previous chapters have demonstrated, Chaucer's objective in *Boece* is to produce a close but intelligible translation. Indeed, he is clearly writing for an audience which wishes a translation of the *Consolation*, not an adaptation. He avoids constructions which are alien to English and employs a variety of techniques, such as doublets and expansions of participles, in order to present the meaning of the *Consolation* as accurately as possible. By disregarding these aspects of *Boece* and focusing on the scattered examples of literary artistry—e.g. alliteration and rhythm—critics have misrepresented the style of

Chaucer's translation. That is, they have presumed that these examples indicate a uniform stylistic level that Chaucer intended for the entire translation, and if this is the case, then *Boece* must be considered a stylistic failure. But the style of *Boece* cannot be assessed in this traditional way, for its lexical and syntactic techniques reveal that aesthetic considerations are incidental in Chaucer's procedure. In *Boece*, style is limited to the expression of meaning. Whether the style of a particular Latin or French passage is colloquial or elevated, Chaucer responds to the passage in the same way: he attempts to express its meaning as accurately as possible. All of Chaucer's techniques — his use of the French, his combined use of the French and Latin, and his original contributions — are conditioned by his concern over meaning. To be sure, there are passages which can be considered stylistically successful in the traditional sense. But, as this chapter will argue, it is possible to evaluate the style of a given Middle English passage only by comparing the passage with the grammatical and intellectual complexity of its Latin and French sources.

Throughout the previous chapters it has been shown that much of Chaucer's lexicon and syntax is indebted to the French. This use of the French in accordance with his own objectives is also apparent in passages of idiomatic or intellectually complex Latin. By idiomatic Latin, simple idioms, such as "morem gerere," are not intended here. Rather, the idiom of a language is its peculiar phraseology. The idiom of Latin is its peculiar way of saying something, which occasionally is not the Old French or Middle English way. For example, there are certain Latin constructions which, unlike grammatical shibboleths, when imitated in Middle English can be perfectly grammatical, intelligible, and unexceptionable. However, there are also sometimes native English constructions which are more idiomatic than simple imitations of the Latin. In the previous chapter Chaucer's imitations — his syntactic derivatives — were discussed; here it will be appropriate to consider his substitutions of native English structures, for these substitutions reflect one of Chaucer's apparent stylistic concerns — that his translation be close yet as idiomatic as possible. Since Jean naturalized much of the idiomatic Latin of the *Consolatio*, and since the idiom of Old French has much in common with that of Middle English, Chaucer frequently avoids the Latin idiom by imitating the French naturalizations. In effect, he substitutes the English idiom, via the French, for the Latin. For example:

> ne latere posteros queat (1p4.75)
> pour ce que cil qui vivront aprés nous la puissent savoir (88)[1]
> for as moche as folk that been to comen aftir our dayes schullen knowen it (168-69)

> non quo uoluntas peteret (2p1.48-49)
> non pas la ou tu voudroies (55)
> nat thider that thow woldest (103)

> Quodsi putatis longius uitam trahi (2m7.23)
> Et se vous cuidéz plus longuement vivre (15)
> And yif ye wene to lyve the longer (26-27)

> sed cum tui muneris sit (4p6.1)
> mais comme tu m'aiez donné ou promis (1)
> But so as thou has yeven or byhyght (1-2)

> Sed quoniam haec quoque... nosse (4p6.12-13)
> Mais pour ce que la cognoissance de ces chosez (16)
> But for as moche as the knowynge of thise thinges (31-32)

In Latin, human agents are frequently expressed in the oblique cases, whereas in Old French and Middle English it is more common to make the human agent the subject of the sentence. Thus, in the first and fourth examples, the Latin is restructured so that "posteros" and "tui," respectively, become the subjects, while in the second example a human subject is inferred from the Latin. An infinitive functioning as the subject of a sentence is also characteristic of the Latin idiom, as is a direct object phrase such as "uitam trahi," and so Chaucer follows Jean in substituting expressions which are more natural in his own language. The avoidance of non-human subjects is apparent in a variety of other phrases, such as:

> esset ascensus (1p1.19)
> l'en peust monter (20)
> men myghten clymben (35)

> In quo illud est animaduertendum magis (3p4.20)
> En quoy ce doit on plus regarder (21-22)
> And yet men aughten taken more heede in this (43-44)

This tendency to restructure the Latin idiom can produce what are, strictly speaking, mistranslations. For example:

> Eandem tamen uestem uiolentorum quorundam sciderant manus (1p1.19-20)
> Et toutevois les mains d'aucunes gens avoient tranchié cele robe par force et par violence (20-22)
> Natheles handes of some men hadden korve that cloth by violence and by strengthe (36-38)

> terras perosa despicit (4m1.4)
> elle despit les terrez haineuses (2)
> it despiseth the hateful erthes (4)

But it is important to note that although "by violence and by strengthe" and "hateful erthes" are mistranslations, the meanings of the passages are not significantly altered. In the first example, it is even perhaps more vivid to speak of "men who act by means of violence" rather than of "violent men"; and in the second passage, there is little semantic difference between "hateful thought despises the earth" and "thought despises the earth which excites hate in it." Thus, Jean and Chaucer have restructured the Latin expressions into Old French and Middle English expressions which are perhaps more, and certainly no less, vivid than the originals.

Chaucer's stylistic technique of following the French in passages of idiomatic Latin is particularly evident in many of the "metra," where the Latin lexicon and syntax can be especially convoluted or elliptical:

> Si quantas rapidis flatibus incitus / pontus uersat harenas / aut quot stelliferis edita noctibus / caelo sidera fulgent / tantas fundat opes nec retrahat manum / pleno Copia cornu (2m2.1-6)
> Se l'abundance, la deesse des richeces donnoit aus hommes a plaine corne sans retraire sa main autant de richeces comme la mer tournoie poudres de gravelles quant elle est esmeue par ravissable vent, ou autant comme il resplendist ou ciel des estoilles luisans par les cleres nuiz (1-4)

> Though Plente (that is, goddesse of rychesses) hielde adoun with ful horn, and withdraweth nat hir hand, as many richesses as the see torneth upward sandes whan it is moeved with ravysshynge blastes, or elles as manye rychesses as ther schynen bryghte sterres in hevene on the sterry nyghtes (1-7)

Boethius is being consciously rhetorical here; he suspends the main clause and uses complex and poetic subordinate clauses. Although Chaucer does not translate the French word-for-word, he does take several lexical derivatives from it and follows Jean in fronting the main clause — a clause order which is more idiomatic for Old French and Middle English.

One of Chaucer's most common techniques in translating idiomatic Latin is to use Jean's general restructuring of the Latin as the basis for his own further naturalizations. For example:

> quid...placet (2p6.9-10)
> quelle autre chose a il...bele et plaisant (11)
> what aggreable thynges is (22)
>
> qui tempus ab aeuo / ire iubes (3m9.2-3)
> qui commandez que li temps aille de pardurableté (des lors que aagez out commencement) (2-3)
> that comaundest the tymes to gon from syn that age hadde bygynnynge (3-5)
>
> sine quo uoluntatis miserae langueret effectus (4p4.11-12)
> car sens le pooir la chetive volenté ne vendroit jamais au fait (13-14)
> withoute which mowynge the wrecchid wil scholde langwisse withouten effect (26-27)

In the first passage, Chaucer follows Jean in substituting a native, idiomatic phrase for the characteristically Latin "quid placet," but avoids Jean's tautological doublet; while in the second, Chaucer imitates the French expansion of the concise "ab aeuo" but eliminates the unnecessary "de pardurableté." The final example suggests another of Jean's (and Chaucer's) common techniques: the transference of a semantically important noun into the subject position. In this case, "uoluntatis miserae" is transferred from the genitive to the nominative case, but Jean's treatment of the verb and of "effectus," the former subject, is inexact. Chaucer improves the French translation with two lexical derivatives.

Characteristic of idiomatic Latin is the ellipsis of verbs and nouns. Context almost always suggest what the reader is meant to understand, but these elliptical constructions are not as pervasive in Old French prose as they are in Latin, and so Jean frequently supplies the understood verb or noun. Given his interest in meaning, Chaucer almost invariably supplies the understood words, too. In the first example below, the Latin establishes a comparison, and the finite verb "obduxerat" occurs in the next clause; thus, Jean and Chaucer supply an infinitive with the same meaning. In the second example, "est" occurs in a preceding, parallel clause, but "unde" sufficiently suggests what verb is to be supplied:

> solet (1p1.15)
> seult occurcir (15)
> is wont to dirken (27)
>
> unde mala (1p4.90)
> dom viennent li mal (106)
> whennes comen wikkide thyngis (200-201)

The following passage indicates still another common stylistic feature of Jean's and Chaucer's translations: the repetition of a verb which is used once in the Latin for parallel clauses. In this case, several clauses which describe what does not disturb the man who disregards fate are terminated with "mouebit." Jean and Chaucer, however, repeat the verb in the middle of the parallel series. Although such a repetition destroys the rhetorical artistry of Boethius's periodic sentence, it does result in more natural Old French and Middle English than simple imitation of the Latin would:

> non illum rabies minaeque ponti / uersum funditus exagitantis aestum / nec ruptis quotiens uagus caminis / torquet fumificos Vesaeuus ignes / aut celsas soliti ferire turres / ardentis uia fulminis mouebit (1m4.5-10)
> la rage et les menaces de la mer demenant, sa bouture tornee du fons jusques en hault, n'esmouvra pas celui; ne Vesevus, foloiable montaigne, toutez les foiz que il tornoie fues fumans par ses cheminees rumpues, ne voie de foudre ardant acoustumee de ferir les hautes tourz, ne le mouvra pas (3-7)

> The rage ne the manaces of the see, commoevynge or chasynge upward hete fro the botme, ne schal nat moeve that man. Ne the unstable mowntaigne that highte Visevus, that writhith out thurw his brokene chemeneyes smokynge fieres, ne the wey of thondernleit, that is wont to smyten hye toures, ne schal not moeve that man (5-12)

This technique of repeating words is particularly common with nouns, for in the Latin idiom, since Latin is a synthetic language, pronouns are frequently sufficient where nouns are clearer and more natural in Old French and Middle English. For example:

> hanc (1m3.7)
> celle nuit (6)
> this nyght (13)
>
> De quibus (2p6.45)
> Des quiex dons (49)
> Of the whiche yiftes (91-92)
>
> haec (3p8.29)
> cist bien mondain (30)
> thise worldly goodes (56-57)

Chaucer and Jean also frequently repeat a noun which is used only once in the Latin in a parallel construction:

> Diuitiaene uel uestrae uel sui natura pretiosae sunt (2p5.6)
> Richeces sont elles precieuses ou par la nature de vous ou par la nature de elles meismes (5-7)
> Richesses ben they preciouse by the nature of hemself, or elles by the nature of the (8-10)

Jefferson (1917:33) criticizes Chaucer's substitution of nouns for pronouns as follows:

> Chaucer seems to have thought that the principle of clearness demanded that the reader be constantly reminded of the name of the thing written about. Accordingly in any given passage we are likely to find a somewhat monotonous repetition of the principal noun, avoided in the Latin by the frequent use of pronouns.

This is a rather puzzling criticism. First, it contradicts one of Jefferson's other complaints about Chaucer's style—the excessive use of "that," which was discussed in the previous chapter. Second, it is self-contradictory; it acknowledges Chaucer's desire for clarity, but then criticizes him for attempting to realize it. And third, it disregards the fundamental differences between Latin and Middle English. Boethius had a highly inflected set of pronouns at his disposal; Chaucer did not. Had Chaucer used pronouns whenever Boethius did, *Boece* would be filled with "thats" and "whiches" the references of which would be uncertain. The pronoun system of Old French is more precise than that of Middle English, and so Chaucer occasionally expands Jean's treatment, too:

> Quorum (1p4.48)
> du nombre des quiex (58)
> Of the nombre of whiche accusours (111-12)

One final example of Chaucer's use of the French in responding to the Latin idiom will suffice:

> quodam loco (2p7.27)
> en un sien livre (31)
> in his book (60)

In this passage, Lady Philosophy is paraphrasing Cicero, and she uses the conventional "locus" to describe the source of the quotation.[2] Yet, Cicero was quite obviously a writer, and so rather than imitate the Latin convention — which Boethius has perhaps included for stylistic reasons and which would be simply imprecise in Old French and Middle English — Chaucer and Jean, who generally is not as concerned as Chaucer with meaning, respond with the precise "book" and "livre."

It is also an aspect of Chaucer's style to follow the French in intellectually complex passages. In such passages, although the Latin idiom by itself may present no problems, the ideas of the passage are complex, and in such cases Chaucer frequently uses the convenience of Jean's translation. For example:

> Neque enim sensus aliquid extra materiam ualet uel uniuersales species imaginatio contuetur uel ratio capit simplicem formam (5p4.83-85)
> Car sens ne puet nulle chose comprendre hors de matere, ne l'imaginacion ne regarde pas les especez universelez, ne raison ne comprent pas la simple forme, si comme intelligence la prent (95-98)

> For wit ne mai no thing comprehende out of matere ne the ymaginacioun ne loketh nat the universels speces, ne resoun ne taketh nat the symple forme so as intelligence takith it (174-78)[3]

Lady Philosophy is here speaking of epistemology, and the intellectual complexity of the passage is undeniable. The similarities between Chaucer's and Jean's translations are striking; not only does Chaucer employ lexical and syntactic derivatives, he imitates Jean's translation of "extra" and copies the French word order to such an extent that every negative and article in the French has an equivalent in the English. In the following passage, Boethius is arguing against the existence of free will, the topic on which Book Five centers. Here Chaucer follows Jean in inserting an introductory clause, changing the datives of the next clause into genitives, adding the conjunction "syn that," expanding "prospiciens" into a finite verb and postposing the adverbial phrase, and emphasizing the idea of the sentence with "by necessite":

> Quare nulla est humanis consiliis actionibusque libertas, quas diuina mens sine falsitatis errore cuncta prospiciens ad unum alligat et constringit euentum (5p3.73-76)
>
> Par quoy il s'ensuit que la franchise des consuez et des euvrez humaines est nulle, puis que la pensee de dieu qui toutez chosez voit sens erreur de fausseté les lie et contraint a un avenement par neccessité (81-84)
>
> For which it folweth that the fredom of the conseiles and of the werkis of mankynde nis noon, syn that the thought of God, that seeth alle thinges withouten errour of falsnesse, byndeth and constreyneth hem to a bytidynge by necessite (144-49)

Before concluding this discussion of Chaucer's use of the French, brief mention should be made of the times when Chaucer does not follow Jean's translation. One of the most striking characteristics of Jean's translation is its wordiness. Although *Boece* may be "diffuse," it is diffuse with a purpose: to express the ideas of the *Consolation*. Jean's translation, on the other hand, is frequently diffuse to no apparent end. He elaborates on intellectually and grammatically simple passages and makes redundant additions. For example:

Estne aliquid tibi te ipso pretiosius (2p4.65-66)
Est il nulle chose que tu plus aimes et tiengnes pour plus chiere que toy meismes (76-77)
Is there anythyng more precyous to the than thiself (132-33)

Aetate...M. Tullii (2p7.26)
au temps que vivoit Marcus Tullius (30)
in the tyme of Marcus Tulyus (58-59)

imbecilles (4p2.37)
foible et non puissant (38-39)
feble (80)

indignum esse si scientiae dei causam futura nostra praestare dicantur (5p6.140-42)
il n'est pas digne chose de dire que nos futurs doignent cause a la science de dieu ne que il soient cause de celle prescience (159-61)
it is unworthy thing to seyn that our futures yeven cause of the science of God (281-82)

The verb phrases Jean inserts in the first two examples do nothing to clarify the sentences, while his additions in the last two examples are simply redundant. Doublets, whether of words or clauses, which consist of a translation of the Latin and the negation of its antonym, as in the third example, are pervasive in Jean's translation. While such doublets do occur as stylistic ornaments in late medieval prose, Chaucer's general avoidance of them indicates, again, that he valued the semantic more than the ornamental potential of doublets. This preference is one of the major stylistic differences between his and Jean's translations. Indeed, Chaucer is particularly adept at taking the good from Jean's translation and leaving the bad, as in the following passage:

acceptaque contumelia (2p7.65)
quant il out receu les outragez et les hontez que cil li ot faitez ou ditez (72-73)
whan he hadde resceyved wordes of outrage (133-34)

Chaucer follows Jean in expanding the ablative absolute and draws lexical derivatives from the French, but he avoids the tautological doublet "les outragez et les hontez" and the useless final clause.

One of the most noteworthy stylistic features of *Boece* is the way in which the Latin and French sources are combined. Doublets formed on the Latin and French are simple examples of this technique, but many long passages show Chaucer moving back and forth between his sources, picking the expressions which seem to him, one presumes, clearest and most contextually appropriate. For example:

> Neque enim ab deminutis inconsummatisque natura rerum cepit exordium, sed ab integris absolutisque procedens in haec extrema atque effeta dilabitur (3p10.14-16)
> Car la nature des chosez ne prist son commencement des chosez amenuisies et non parfaitez, ainçois vient des chosez enterines et delivrez et descent en ces derrenieres chosez foraines et sens fruit (14-17)
> For the nature of thinges ne took nat hir begynnynge of thinges amenused and inparfit, but it procedith of thinges that ben alle hole and absolut, and descendith so doun into uttereste thinges and into thinges empty and withouten fruyt (25-30)

Here Chaucer has lexical derivatives from both the French — "amenused," "inparfit" and "descendith" — and the Latin — "procedith" and "absolut." He has followed Jean in turning "procedens" into a finite verb and juxtaposing it with his translation of "dilabitur," but, unlike Jean, he is careful to indicate that "extrema" and "effeta" refer to two different things. The following is a much simpler example of Chaucer blending lexical derivatives — in the final phrase, his adjective is from the French, while his noun is from the Latin:

> hic portus placida manens quiete (3m10.5)
> ci est li pors establez en pesible repons (3)
> her is the havene stable in pesible quiete (5-6)

Another common type of combined translation involves a series of clauses closely translated from the French and one translated from the Latin. Generally, as in the following passage, the initial French clauses are good translations, but for the clause which is taken directly from the Latin, the French is inaccurate:

> Cuncta quae rara prouehit aetas / stupetque subitis mobile uulgus, / cedat inscitiae nubilus error, / cessent profecto mira uideri (4m5.19-22)
>
> Li mouvablez peuples s'esbahist et se merveille de toutez les chosez qui aviennent tardivez et soudaines en nostre aage. Mais se la trouble erreur de nostre ignorance se departist de nous, se que nous seussons les causez pour quoy tiex chosez aviennent, certainement nous ne verrions jamés merveilles avenir (15-19)
>
> The moevable peple is astoned of alle thinges that comen seelde and sodeynly in our age; but yif the trubly errour of our ignoraunce departed fro us, so that we wisten the causes why that swiche thinges bytyden, certes thei scholde cesen to seme wondres (30-36)

Chaucer's translation of the first three lines of the Latin is taken almost word-for-word from the French; he follows the French rearrangement of the first two clauses, takes several lexical derivatives from the French and includes both the small clarifications which Jean makes (e.g. "in our age") and his long inference. But in the last clause, perhaps misled by "uideri," Jean has drastically and ineffectively restructured the Latin. Hence, Chaucer translates Boethius and even takes the lexical derivative "cesen."

Perhaps the most unusual way by which Chaucer combines the Latin and French is through what might be called double translations. That is, he first translates the Latin and then translates the French translation of it, generally by disguising the second translation as a gloss with "that is to seyn" or "as who seith." For the most part, some small semantic distinction is thus achieved, but the passages nonetheless tend to strike the reader as redundant and to slow down the course of the narrative. The passages which Chaucer translates twice may consist of phrases or of single words, in which case all that distinguishes them from doublets is the glossarial introduction to the second word. For example:

> intra fortunae aream (2p1.44)
> en cest monde (50)
> inwith the floor of Fortune (that is to seyn, in this world) (93-94)
>
> suo fonte (4m6.43)
> de leur commencement (27)
> from hir welle (that is to seyn, from hir bygynnynge) (52-53)

> facultatem (5p4.68)
> le pooir et la nature (78-79)
> the faculte (that is to seyn, the power and the nature) (141-42)

In the first two examples, Jean's translations are less poetic than the Latin originals, while in the final example, Chaucer uses Jean's translation as a gloss on the philosophically complex "facultas."

In the following example of a double translation of a phrase, there seems to be little semantic difference between the Latin and French:

> quicumque in superum diem / mentem ducere quaeritis (3m12.53-54)
> quiconques couvoitiés metre vostre pensee en la tres grant clarté du souverain bien (32-33)
> whosoevere desireth or seketh to lede his thought into the sovereyn day (that is to seyn, to cleernesse of sovereyne good) (61-63)

Robinson (1957:806) notes, "Chaucer's gloss here combines that of Trivet, 'in superna bona,' and that of the Pseudo-Aquinas, 'in supernam claritatem.'" However, Chaucer's "gloss" is simply a translation of the French translation of "supernum diem." The French version is perhaps less poetic than the Latin, but Chaucer's double translation does not seem necessary. Finally, double translations may also involve entire clauses, as in the following passage:

> illa quoque noscendi uices alternare uideatur (5p6.132-33)
> ne nous doit pas estre avis que elle entrechange aussi ses divers fais de cognoistre si que elle cognoisse une foiz une chose et autre foiz le contraire de ce (149-51)
> And thilke prescience—ne semeth it nat to entrechaunge stoundis of knowynge? (As who seith, ne schal it nat seme to us that the devyne prescience entrechaungith his diverse stoundes of knowynge, so that it knowe somtyme o thing, and somtyme the contrarie?) (261-66)[4]

In some cases, Chaucer omits the glossarial bridge between the translations—an omission which both obscures their syntactic relationship and clearly reveals that they constitute a double translation:

> Sed quantum ornamentis nostris decesserit, uides (2p4.31-32)
> Mais tu vois combien il fault de honneur a nos aournemens (37-38)

> but thou mayst wel seen how grete apparailes and array that me lakketh, that ben passed awey fro me (61-63)

> uelut hydrae capita succrescant (4p6.7-8)
> aussi comme croissoient les testes au serpent que Herculez occist (9-10)
> ryght as the hevedes waxen of Idre (the serpent that Hercules slowh) (18-20)

The first passage is somewhat unusual, in that it is the French translation — "me lakketh" from "il fault" — which is "glossed" with the Latin. In the second passage, the second translation is a useful gloss of "Idre" — both the *OED* and the *MED* cite *Boece* for the earliest occurrence of the word — and, syntactically, is easily interpreted as standing in apposition to the first translation. In the first passage, however, the difference between the translations is simply stylistic, and the juxtaposition of them is rather awkward. Such double translations recall the doublets whose "raison d'être" seems to be only the idiomatic differences between the Latin and French and are thus another indication of Chaucer's interest in the manipulation of language. The double translations are scattered throughout *Boece*, and there seems to be no real reason — semantic or grammatical — for many of them. Moreover, the double translations indicate just how little Chaucer was interested in style in the traditional sense. For instance, the double translation of an entire clause which was quoted above demonstrates no concern for proportion or the continuity of the argument. The double translations are an important part of Chaucer's style in *Boece*, but they are certainly unstylish, in the modern sense.

The perception of style as meaning in *Boece* is also apparent in a variety of techniques which Chaucer uses independently of the French. Chaucer generally naturalizes idiomatic Latin, for instance, when Jean does not. Chaucer also uses a more diverse selection of glosses than does Jean, as well as several other techniques which may retard the progress of the argument but are indicative of his concern for meaning.

The passive voice is much more common in the idiom of Latin than in the idiom of Middle English. Moreover, the passive voice is especially common in the *Consolatio*, since the passive voice is a prominent aspect of argumentative prose in Latin. Although Chaucer does imitate the construction, he also quite frequently restructures it into an expression more characteristic of the Middle English idiom. For example:

> quanto mouereris cachinno (2p6.15-16)
> de con grans escharnissemens seroies tu esmeus (18-19)
> how gret scorn woldestow han of it (34-35)

Another aspect of Chaucer's style is his occasional preference for active—in a figurative sense—constructions, as in the following passage:

> securus esse desistis (2p5.92)
> tu delaissez a estre seurs (110)
> thanne hastow lorn thi sikernesse (187-88)

When Jean imitates the Latin by leaving verbs or nouns in ellipsis, Chaucer generally supplies the understood words. In the first example below, Boethius uses a modal and leaves the infinitive to be inferred—characteristic of the Latin idiom—while Chaucer includes the understood infinitive. And in the second example, Chaucer supplies a finite verb which nicely completes the parallel Boethius establishes.

> potuit (1p1.21)
> pot (22)
> hy myghte geten (40)

> famem satient . . . sitim frigusque depellant (3p3.43-44)
> il saoulent leur fain et ostent la soif et le froit (48)
> thei mai staunchen hir hungir, and slaken hir thurst, and don awey cold (87-88)

Chaucer regularly supplies understood nouns for pronouns and for substantival adjectives:

> quibus (1p1.18)
> par lesquiex (19-20)
> by whiche degrees (34-35)

> In quibus (1p3.23-24)
> Et en yceus (23)
> In whiche Epycuriens and Stoyciens (44)

lenioribus (1p5.35)
plus legiers (39)
lyghtere medicynes (73)

ea perspecta (3p1.21)
quant tu auras regardé celle (26)
whanne thow hast fully byhoolden thilke false goodes (47-48)

In some cases, as in the following passage, Chaucer interpolates a noun or verb in order to clarify or emphasize a parallel Boethius is drawing. Some critics—to be discussed later—have taken such a technique as an indication of Chaucer's desire for balanced phrasing; that is, the technique is regarded as an aspect of Chaucer's artistic style. But it is equally possible, and more in harmony with the other features of Chaucer's style, to cite Chaucer's desire for clarity as the motivation for the interpolated words.

> non morte solum uerum etiam doloribus suppliciisque (2p4.86-87)
> non mie tant seulement par mort, mais neis par douleurs et par tourmens (100-101)
> nat oonly with suffrynge of deeth, but eek with suffrynge of peynes and tormentz (178-80)

By twice inserting "suffrynge," Chaucer emphasizes the parallel between the two clauses and develops the notion of "deeth," "peynes" and "tormentz" as constituting experiences.

Occasionally, Chaucer's concern with clarifying pronoun references leads him into interpolating the wrong noun. For instance:

> An ignoras illam tuae ciuitatis antiquissimam legem qua sanctum est ei ius exsulare non esse quisquis in ea sedem fundare maluerit (1p5.12-14)
> As tu donques oublié ou ne sces tu pas celle tres anciene loy de ta cité par la quelle il est jugiés que quiconques voudra mieux ileuc fonder son siege et sa maison que ailleurs, il n'en a pooir de estre exilliéz (14-16)
> Hastow foryeten thilke ryght oolde lawe of thi citee, in the whiche cite it es ordeyned and establysschid, that what wyght that hath levere founden therein his sete or his hous than elleswhere, he may nat ben exiled by no ryght fro that place (25-31)

> an sit eorum aliquid quod beatitudinis substantiam compleat, ad hoc uero cetera referantur (3p10.84-85)

101

> ou, savoir mon, se aucune de toutez ycelles soit telle que elle acomplisse par soi la sustance de beneurté, si que toutez ces chosez autres soient raportees a lui (92-94)
>
> or elles yif ony of alle thilke thinges ben swich that it acomplise by himself the substaunce of blisfulnesse, so that alle thise othere thynges ben referrid and brought to blisfulnesse (that is to seyn, as to the cheef of hem) (163-67)

In the first passage, Chaucer's "in the whiche" is incorrect, for "qua" is an ablative of means referring to "legem." And in the second passage, the Latin "ad quod" refers to "aliquid." Chaucer apparently misconstrues it with "beatitudinis," although his gloss is ambiguous.

In general, however, Chaucer's technique of interpolating nouns is quite effective. He uses it to clarify not only substantival adjectives and pronouns, but also unfamiliar terms and abstract nouns. For example, in the first passage below the interpolated noun specifies which part of her gown Lady Philosophy uses to dry Boethius's eyes; and in the second, Chaucer's noun develops the figurative sense in which "lucem" is being used.

> ueste (1p2.15)
> par sa robe (14)
> with the lappe of hir garnement (27-28)
>
> lucem (3m10.17)
> clarté (13)
> light of blisfulnesse (26-27)

Chaucer also frequently interpolates entire clauses which are understood in the Latin and French, as in the following passage, where Lady Philosophy has just asked Boethius if there is anything which "deo contra ire conetur" and Boethius has answered "Nihil." She continues:

> Quodsi conetur (3p12.49)
> Et se riens...s'i esforçoit (50-51)
> And yif that any thing enforcede hym to withstonde God (106-107)

Chaucer's glosses are perhaps the most noticeable feature of his style in *Boece*, particularly so because in Robinson's edition, the standard edition, all the glossarial passages are intended to be italicized. Some of these passages are derived from French expansions, some from Nicholas Trevet's commentary and Remigius of Auxerre's glosses to the *Consolatio*, and some are Chaucer's own contributions.[5] Silk (1930:42) was of the opinion that, in essence, the entire *Boece* is derived from Trevet's commentary: "Trivet's commentary was Chaucer's chief, perhaps, his sole tool in executing his translation of Boethius." To be sure, this is a misrepresentation of the situation. There is no doubt that Chaucer used Trevet's commentary. But for the most part he draws on it only for glosses and seldom for words or phrases of the text itself:

> Sed cur tanto flagrat amore / ueri tectas reperire notas? / Scitne quod appetit anxia nosse (5m3.11-13)
> Mais pour quoy s'eschaufe elle par si grant desirier a trouver les couvertez notez de verité? Scet elle que elle ait cogneu ce que elle requiert angoisseusement a cognoistre (11-13)
> But wherfore eschaufeth it so by so gret love to fynden thilke notes of soth icovered? (That is to seyn, wherfore eschaufeth the thought of man by so gret desir to knowen thilke notificaciouns that ben ihid undir the covertures of soth?) Woot it aught thilke thing that it angwisshous desireth to knowe? (As who seith, nay; for no man ne travaileth for to witen thingis that he wot. And therfore the texte seith thus:) (17-27)
> SED CUR FLAGRAT id est ardet, hoc est ardenter cupit, scilicet anima REPERIRE NOTAS id est notificaciones TECTAS id est latentes obscuritate VERI id est veritatis SCITNE id est numquid dicendum est quod scit illud QUOD ANXIA APPETIT NOSSE? quasi diceret non, quia nullus appetit scire illud, quod scit unde subdit. (Trevet, 711)

Chaucer's translation of the Latin text itself is lexically and syntactically indebted to the French. The glosses which interpret and explain the text, however, are clearly derived from Trevet. Thus, Trevet's glosses are evidence not for Chaucer's *translation* of the *Consolatio*—as Silk argued—but for his *interpretation* of it. Chaucer very likely would not agree with this distinction between Boethius's text and the Latin glosses on it. Indeed, as the final chapter will suggest, Chaucer's procedure indicates that he viewed the *Consolation* as, in effect, a composite endeavor:

Boethius's *Consolatio*, Jean de Meung's translation, Trevet's commentary and Remigius of Auxerre's glosses. Nonetheless, Chaucer does in practice distinguish between the Latin text and the French translation and glosses, for while he will incorporate French glosses and contextually appropriate expansions — understood words and the like — he tends to avoid Jean's additions to the Latin text itself and to focus on the *Consolatio* when Jean abridges it.

One of Chaucer's most common glossarial techniques is to use one of Jean's expansions as a gloss on the Latin text:

> Sed quoniam id eis non propria uis sed hominum fallax adnectit opinio (3p4.32-33)
> Mais pour ce que ce ne leur vient pas de leur propre nature, mais seulement de la fausse cuidance des hommes qui cuident que les dignitéz les facent dignes (34-36)
> But for as mochel as for to be holden honourable or reverent ne cometh nat to folk of hir propre strengthe of nature, but oonly of the false opynyoun of folk (that is to seyn, that weenen that dignytees maken folk digne of honour) (69-74)

> uiuacissimo mentis igne (4p6.9)
> par tres vivable feu de pensee et par vigueur d'engin (11)
> by a ryght lifly and quyk fir of thought (that is to seyn, by vigour and strengthe of wit) (22-24)

Chaucer's glosses also occasionally consist of a combination of Jean's translation and Trevet's commentary:

> summam et singula (5m3.21)
> la somme des chosez et chascune par soy (19)
> the somme and the singularites (that is to seyn, the principles and everych by hymself) (40-42)
> SUMMAM id est principia PARITER ET SINGULA id est conclusiones in principiis (Trevet, 713)

Although Chaucer's glosses demonstrate his concern for meaning, they do not seem to have been applied in a systematic fashion. Many passages of complex ideas are glossed, but others are not. And some glosses, such as that at 4p6.22-24, which was cited above, are not especially insightful. The glosses, particularly those from Trevet, occur more frequently in Books Four and

Five, where the intellectual content of the *Consolatio* becomes increasingly complex. They are especially common in the "metra" of the later Books, for these contain many mythological and literary allusions which Jean generally does not explain. Furthermore, Jean has a tendency to abridge the difficult parts of the "metra," and so Chaucer, with his desire for accuracy, had to consult Trevet more frequently for them. An exhaustive study of Chaucer's glosses is certainly outside the scope of this book, but it is important to point out, by way of conclusion, that, like the double translations, the abundance of glosses in *Boece* indicates that Chaucer was much more concerned with meaning than with artistic style.

Before concluding this chapter, a few miscellaneous aspects of Chaucer's style should be noted. First, Chaucer regularly identifies proper nouns as such by explaining that they refer to a man, mountain, or whatever.[6] Jean provided the inspiration for some of these identifications, but the majority can be attributed solely to Chaucer. For example:

> praecipiti...Coro (1m3.3)
> par Chorus qui est un vent ineaus (3)
> by a swift wynde that hyghte Chorus (6-7)

> Threicio (1m3.7)
> treicienne (6)
> of the cuntre of Trace (12-13)

> uagus...Vesaeuus (1m4.7-8)
> Vesevus, foloiable montaigne (5)
> the unstable mowntaigne that highte Visevus (8-9)

> Conigastum (1p4.28)
> Congaste (31)
> thilke man that highte Conigaste (55-56)

> Sirius (1m5.22)
> Sirius (15)
> the sterre Syrius (28)

Another one of Chaucer's stylistic techniques which is designed to clarify the meaning of a given passage is the use of "that is to seyn" to set off nouns or clauses in apposition. The Latin idiom

TECHNIQUES OF TRANSLATION

allows for such juxtaposition, but the construction can be somewhat vague in Old French and Middle English, and, for the most part, Chaucer uses the separating clause on the inspiration of the French translation.

> quibus hoc maxime propositum est, pessimis displicere (1p3.33-34)
> aux quiex meismement li propos est itiex, c'est a savoir desplaire aus tres mauvais (34-35)
> In the whiche tempestes this is my moste purpoos, that is to seyn to displesen to wikkede men (65-67)

> Habes igitur ante oculos propositam fere formam felicitatis humanae: opes, honores, potentiam, gloriam, uoluptates (3p2.40-42)
> Donques as tu devant tes yeulz proposee pres que toute la forme de la beneurté humaine, c'est a savoir richeces, honneurs, puissances, gloirez, deliz (43-45)
> Now hastow thanne byforn thyne eien almest al the purposede forme of the welefulnesse of mankynde: that is to seyn rychesses, honours, power, glorie, and delitz (74-77)

One final feature of Chaucer's style in *Boece* is the use of cleft sentences, or empty introductory clauses. Most often he uses this construction at the beginning of a description of a hypothetical situation—as if to stress that the following statement has not been established as fact—although the construction introduces simple, declarative sentences as well. Jean does not use the construction as frequently as Chaucer, and the phrases seem to achieve no semantic clarification either in the French or in the English. Indeed, of all Chaucer's lexical, syntactic and stylistic techniques in *Boece*, this seems the most inexplicable. Some examples are:

> Quis non...praedicauit (2p3.17-19)
> qui fu cil qui ne te tint et preescha (19)
> Who is it that ne seide (36)

> Quis est ille tam felix, qui (2p4.56)
> Qui est cil tant beneuréz que (66)
> What man is that that is so weleful (116)

> Nam cum quidam adortus esset (2p7.60)
> Car comme uns homme eust assailli (66-67)[7]
> Whilom ther was a man that hadde assaied (123)

Quodsi (3p3.10)
Mais se (12)
But yif it so be that (17-18)

It is clear, then, that Chaucer's style in *Boece* is directed towards the end of a close but intelligible translation. What Chaucer writes is conditioned not by artistic considerations but by a concern for meaning: to express intellectually complex or idiomatic Latin and French in English. Those critics who have praised the literary artistry of *Boece* have apparently disregarded its most prominent stylistic features: the restructuring of idiomatic Latin, the insertion of understood words, double translations, glosses and the identification of proper nouns. For instance, Stewart (1891:228) claims that there are "instances where [Chaucer] actually reproduces the original Latin metre." But, laying aside Chaucer's concern for meaning and debt to the French, this is simply impossible, because Latin meter is predicated upon the time values of the items involved, while English meter is determined by stress; although it is possible to substitute an analogous stress-pattern for a time-pattern, it is formally impossible to "reproduce" Latin meter in English.[8] In much of the favorable criticism of *Boece*, there is the tacit assumption that somewhere in *Boece* Chaucer the poet is struggling to write poetry. Thus, Root (1934:85) suggests that

> the prose of Chaucer's translation, if not always felicitous, is anything but artless. It employs intricate alliteration, balance and antithesis, varied cadence of clause, and other 'colours of rethoryk.'

Baum (1946) has cited examples of blank verse in *Boece*, while Skeat (1900:xxiii) has pointed out one of the best rhythmical passages in the translation:

> It liketh me to shewe by subtil soong,
> With slakke and delytable sown of strenges
> (3m2.1-2)[9]

There are also passages where Chaucer has quite obviously introduced alliteration:

> et eo usque cum his quos eludere nititur blandissimam habet famil-
> iaritatem (2p1.6-7)[10]
> et comment elle porte tres soueve familiarité et tres habondant amour a
> ceulz que elle s'esforce a decevoir (7-8)
> and how sche useth ful flaterynge famylarite with hem that sche enfor-
> ceth to bygyle (16-18)

And, as Margaret Schlauch contends, Chaucer may make occasional use of cadence in the translation.[11] But it must be stressed how rare such passages are. As the techniques discussed in this and the two previous chapters indicate, Chaucer's style is predominately suited for meaning, so that the passages of literary artistry must be considered incidental in his technique, though they suggest the artistic prose Chaucer would have used had he desired *Boece* to be a "literary" rather than a meaning-oriented translation.[12]

Chaucer's "balance of phrasing" merits further discussion. Jefferson (1917:43) was the first to discuss this aspect of Chaucer's style:

> There is a tendency to be observed throughout the translation for the clauses of a given passage to approach equality in length. Chaucer avoids abrupt and unexpected terminations. This fulness of style is effected by devices such as doubling words in translation... turning phrases of the original into clauses, repeating prominent words such as the subject and predicate in successive clauses.

Cline (1928:95) also notes the "balance of phrasing" and, pointing in particular to the insertion of conjunctions and the repetition of nouns, he suggests that Chaucer wrote *Boece* with the principles of oral delivery in mind and with the aim of constructing isocolonic clauses:

> I have shown that the conventions of 'open' translation conduced to parallelism in the respect that they opened Latin idioms to clauses. In so far as isocolon is a figure of prose, it derives from Latin; yet for all that, it resembles poetry in that it effects a pattern determined not by its intellectual content, nor by its grammatical construction alone, but by the desire of the author

for a recurrent oral effect. This is the desire of the poet; and it is by the methods of poetry that Chaucer intensifies his pattern.

Cline cites the following passage as an example:

> non modo fama hominum singulorum sed ne urbium quidem peruenire queat (2p7.25-26)
> ne la renommee des sanglez hommes ne certez neis des citéz n'ont pooir de venir (27-28)
> nat oonly the names of synguler men ne may nat strecchen, but eek the fame of citees ne may nat strecchen (56-58)

Noting Chaucer's conjunctions and repetition of the verb phrase, Cline (1928:95-96) asserts, "The one certain intention of Chaucer in this sentence was to reflect in his translation the effect — the oral impression — of the Latin — the effect of two similar members unified, yet distinct... It is not that he imitates Latin rhetoric; he writes a style that will stand for it."

Yet, must this be the case? Is it not more logical to conclude that the conjunctions and verbs serve to clarify and emphasize the meaning of this passage? Indeed, as was discussed in the last chapter and earlier in this one, this seems to be the function which most of Chaucer's conjunctions and repeated words serve. Thus, although there certainly is "balance of phrasing" in *Boece*, it is more likely to be a means towards Chaucer's goals of clarity and the manipulation of language rather than an end in itself. Moreover, when there is literary artistry in *Boece*, much of the time it occurs in conjunction with philological artistry. For instance, in the following passages, Chaucer's preservation of the Latin and French word play is both rhetorically and linguistically pleasing:

> ludum ludimus (2p2.26)
> de ce jeu jouons nous (30-31)
> this pley I pleye (50)

> ornari posse aliquid ornamentis... alienis (2p5.79-80)
> riens puisse estre aourné ne enbeli de estranges aournemens (95)
> anythyng mai ben apparailed with straunge apparailementz (159-61)

> ut si quis colendi agri causa fodiens humum defossi auri pondus inueniat (5p1.36-38)

109

> si comme se aucuns foait la terre pour cause de cultiver le champ et trouvast illeques une masse d'or enfoie (39-40)
> Ryght as a man dalf the erthe bycause of tylyinge of the feld, and found there a gobet of gold bydolven (71-73)

This chapter has argued, then, that the style of *Boece* is not literary style in the traditional sense, but style as conditioned by meaning. Chaucer draws on every available resource—Boethius's Latin, Jean's French, Trevet's and Remigius of Auxerre's glosses and his own philological skill— in order to present clearly the meaning of the *Consolation* as he understands it. Moreover, Chaucer evidently had little concern with the proportion or continuity of the argument in the *Consolation*, as his manipulation of language, double translations and extended glosses indicate. The implications of these emphases will be considered in the following chapter.

CHAPTER 5

THE IMPLICATIONS OF CHAUCER'S TECHNIQUE

This [*Religio Medici*] I confesse about seven yeares past, with some others of affinitie thereto, for my private exercise and satisfaction, I had at leisurable houres composed; which being communicated unto one, it became common unto many, and was by transcription successively corrupted untill it arrived in a most depraved copy at the presse. He that shall peruse that worke, and shall take notice of sundry particularities and personall expressions therein, will easily discerne the intention was not publik: and being a private exercise directed to my selfe, what is delivered therein was rather a memoriall unto me than an example or rule unto any other: and therfore if there bee any singularitie therein correspondent unto the private conceptions of any man, it doth not advantage them; or if dissentaneous thereunto, it no way overthrowes them.[1]

At this point in the discussion, before examining *Boece* in further detail, a brief review of the conclusions which have been reached heretofore is appropriate. The first chapter suggested that understanding of *Boece* must begin with recognition of the sources which Chaucer was translating; he was not working from modern editions of the French and Latin but from medieval manuscripts whose texts were not always very good. It is only in relation to such flawed texts that Chaucer's achievement can be assessed. Moreover, he was using fourteenth-century English to compose a translation, not an original work. It is beside the point to suggest, as M. W. Grose (1967:97) does, that "Anyone who wants to read Boethius for his own sake would be better served by a modern translation." The fourteenth-century reader, coming upon a modern translation of the *Consolatio*, would remark, "Anyone who wants to read Boethius for his own sake would be better served by a medieval translation." Chaucer wrote in Middle English for an audience which read Middle English, and, as Chapters Two and Three demonstrated, his lexicon and syntax are generally acceptable according to the standards of fourteenth-century English and (when identifiable) medieval translation. And finally, one of Chaucer's most obvious objectives in *Boece* was to produce a close but intelligible translation. As Chapter Four has emphasized, his translation techniques — such as doublets, calques, lexical and syntactic derivatives, glosses and double translations — are primarily suited to this end, as well as to the end of linguistic manipulation, and not to the end of literary artistry.

With these conclusions in mind, one ought next to ask: What are the implications of Chaucer's technique? Why and for whom did Chaucer prepare such a translation? Why was he interested more in semantic accuracy and philological ingenuity than in literary artistry? Robinson (1957:320), as was noted in Chapter One, suggested that "in passing judgment upon a work of this sort one should remember that literal accuracy rather than the reproduction of stylistic excellence was a recognized ideal of translation in Chaucer's age," but the diversity of medieval translations and current knowledge of medieval translation theory scarcely warrant such a categorical statement. And while Chaucer's translation certainly is "literal," the literalness of the complex doublets and syntactic derivatives is indeed ingenious. Furthermore, it should be noted that *Boece* differs thoroughly from Chaucer's other prose translations, wherein Chaucer clearly is conscious of literary artistry. First, there is the issue of prose style. In *Boece*, as Chapter Four argued, style is the expression of meaning, but each of the other works displays a consistent and appropriate literary style; *Melibee* is notable for its mock-didactic style, the *Parson's Tale* for its colloquial exposition and direct address, and the *Astrolabe* for its distinctively pedagogical tone. Second is the issue of presentation of the material. The rich commentary tradition of the *Consolatio* leads one to expect a proportionately high number of glosses in *Boece*. Yet it is noteworthy that for the most part Chaucer resists breaking up the continuity of the *Parson's Tale* with glosses, even though understanding of its contents was undeniably important for the medieval Christian, and though several diverse versions of Peraldus's and Pennaforte's treatises were available: Chaucer could have used one of the versions as a gloss on another, just as he occasionally used *Li Livres* as a gloss on the *Consolatio*. Finally, with respect to lexicon, the intellectual complexity of the *Consolation* cannot by itself account for the unique vocabulary of *Boece*, for, in its own way, the subject matter of the *Astrolabe* is equally complex. Yet in that translation, as Elliott (1974:135) points out, Chaucer resists the "temptation to import words" from his sources and "is more inclined to make do with English, or at least partly English, equivalents." In *Boece*, however, Chaucer not only imports many words—sometimes, as in doublets on the Latin and French, two at a time—but also uses words in new, extended senses and in unusual forms.

In answer to the question of why Chaucer translated the *Consolation* the way he did, then, one cannot simply say that such a translation was a "recognized ideal" in his day. Literal translation is only one type of medieval translation, and even within the group of what might be considered literal translations, *Boece* may stand alone; Chaucer's technique is considerably more creative than that of the translators of the first Wycliffite Bible, and he takes fewer liberties with his source than does Trevisa with Higden's *Polychronicon*. Nor can one say that Chaucer translated *Boece* the way he did because he was following the norms of translation which obtain in *Melibee*, the *Astrolabe* and the *Parson's Tale*; he was not. In the absence, then, of comparative material, one needs to seek answers to the questions raised above in *Boece* itself. Indeed, there is internal evidence in *Boece* which is relevant to all of the above questions but which hitherto has not been collected. This evidence suggests that *Boece* as we have it had not yet undergone final revision.

First of all, it should be stressed that the lexical experimentation—the nonce words and neologisms—as noted in Chapter Two is not characteristic of a polished translation; a translator cannot afford to indulge his own philological curiosity if he expects his audience to understand and appreciate his translation. While such experimentation does not alter the fact that in general the lexicon of *Boece* is unexceptionable, its presence is still significant. Lexical experimentation, to be sure, can have one of two implications: desperation or creativity. It can imply desperation in that, in the first version of a translation, when a translator temporarily cannot decide which word in his own language is appropriate for the word he is translating, he might adopt a word from his source text or adapt a word from his own language. Thus, a translator of Old English, coming upon the word "wyrd" with its various and complex shades of meaning, might simply use "wyrd" in the first version of his translation. And a translator of Old Icelandic, coming upon the adverb "stórmannliga," might write "big-man-ly." In each case, the translator intends his translation as, in a sense, a note to himself. When he fully understands the context and nuances of the passage, he returns to it and substitutes, perhaps, "fate" or "event" for "wyrd" and "munificently" or "valiantly" for "stórmannliga." Such a procedure may explain some of Chaucer's unusual words. Chaucer knew that "proscripcion," for instance, meant the same as Latin "proscriptio," that "uneschuable" meant "qui n'est pas eschevable," and that "skillynge" meant "the act of reason." He used the words, perhaps, because he was unable to determine immediately the best English equivalents to the Latin and French and intended to return to the passages and substitute more common words.

The other way of interpreting Chaucer's lexical experimentation, the way which has emerged throughout this study, is as an expression of his philological creativity. But even so, it should be noted how many of Chaucer's unusual words are left unexplained. If Chaucer intended *Boece* as we have it for the general reading public, would he not have clarified the meaning of at least the majority of unusual words?[2] Moreover, the distribution of the nonce words and neologisms also suggests that *Boece* did not receive Chaucer's final editorial touches:[3]

	Book 1	Book 2	Book 3	Book 4	Book 5
cols. in Rob. ed.	18	23	33	30	23
nonce words	120	107	108	92	90
no. per col.	6.66	4.65	3.27	3.06	3.91
romance neologisms	61	48	50	42	45
no. per col.	3.38	2.08	1.51	1.40	1.95

The first two Books of the *Consolation* are the simplest intellectually; they essentially are Boethius's narrative of Lady Philosophy's visit to him and of his previous life. The last three Books, on the other hand, which deal with fortune, happiness and free will, become increasingly more philosophically complex. If individual nonce words and neologisms are born of desperation, then the decrease in their numbers suggests a marked improvement in Chaucer's technique; the more he familiarized himself with the *Consolation*, the less need he evidently had for nonce words and neologisms, despite the increasing complexity of the argument. But if this is the case, one would think Chaucer would have returned to the first half of the translation and would have corrected it with his newly acquired skill. If, however, the nonce words and neologisms are born of creativity, one would think that Chaucer would have become increasingly inventive as the argument allowed him more opportunity to use new and unusual words. Yet, as the above chart makes clear, just the opposite holds true: Chaucer is most "creative" in the philosophically simplest Books of the *Consolation*. In other words, the farther he got in the *Consolation*, the more perfunctory Chaucer became, and such a change in technique would also lead one to believe that *Boece* did not undergo final revision: one may suppose that Chaucer, for whatever reason, hurried through the last half of the *Consolation* but intended to return to it and supply it with the same lexical ingenuity as he did the first half. And it is not that the decrease in nonce words and neologisms — whatever their origin — in the later Books is due to the fact that Chaucer is simply reusing words he tried out in the beginning of *Boece*, for 346 of the 517 nonce words, for instance, occur only once (see p. 57).

It is worth noting here that syntactic experimentation, though much less common than lexical experimentation, also occurs in *Boece*. On several occasions Chaucer uses different structures to translate identical syntactic structures occurring within a few lines of each other. For example, one may recall Chaucer's treatment of impersonal Latin verbs with unexpressed subjects. Latin "manifestum est" occurs twice within eleven lines in Book Three, prose ten (see p. 73); Jean translates the phrase the same way both times, but Chaucer first expands it into "men mai seen" and then imitates it with "is it manifest and open." The Latin structures are used in exactly the same way and the passage is short enough that Chaucer could have completed it in a relatively brief time. When imitating the later structure, he almost certainly would remember that he had expanded the earlier one, and so is it possible that his varying treatment is evidence of a conscious attempt to use a wide variety of syntactic structures? Similar variation occurs in the third prose of Book Three, where "egeo" is used five times within fifteen lines in the Latin text. Jean translates the Latin essentially the same way every time — "avoir" and "souffraite" or "mestier" — but Chaucer employs four different constructions:

> Eget...eo (22)
> chascuns a souffraite (24)
> nedeth ther somwhat (41-42)

> Eget (22)
> Souffraite en a il (25)
> Yee, ther nedeth (43)

> Qui...eget aliquo (23)
> cil qui a souffraite de aucune chose (25-26)
> he that hath lak or nede of aught (44-45)

Egebit (34)
aura mestier (38)
hath a man nede (69)

non egeret eo (36)
il n'en eust pas mestier (40)
hym nedide noon help (73-74)

Any of Chaucer's four responses to "egeo" is satisfactory Middle English, and so the use of all four may reflect his sense of — and desire to use — the flexibility of the syntax of his own language as he confronts the syntax of another. Whereas Chaucer's varying treatment of phrases like "manifestum est" and words like "egeo" is almost certainly a conscious technique, it could not be known by — nor be of value to — his readers. In other words, Chaucer's syntactic experimentation, like his lexical experimentation, is a technique which can be appreciated only by a reader who has access to the Latin and French, and such a technique does not seem characteristic of a translation which, in its present form, is intended for the general public.

By themselves the lexical and syntactic experimentation might simply be the marks of a bad translation. More cogent evidence, however, of *Boece* as a first version is provided by what might be called the alternate translations. These passages contain two separate translations of the same clause or sentence, neither of which is based specifically on the Latin or French. Although the second translation of an alternate translation may begin with Chaucer's customary glossarial introductions — and the second translation in all the passages cited herein is italicized by Robinson as if it were a gloss — the differences between the two translations are stylistic and not semantic: both translations say the same thing, and either one is intelligible by itself. For instance, in the following passage Chaucer's first translation is close to the French, which, although it expands "Quis" and "nescius" into clauses, is still quite close to the Latin; the second translation, on the other hand, is more free, expressing the logical implications of the Latin and French. Nevertheless, the first translation is sufficiently clear by itself, and the second translation hardly seems necessary.

> Quis enim quicquam nescius optet (5m3.16)
> Car qui est cil qui desire ce dont il ne scet riens (14-15)
> What is he that desireth any thyng of which he wot right naught? (As who seith, whoso desireth any thing, nedes somwhat he knoweth of it, or elles he coude nat desiren it) (29-33)

In several of Chaucer's alternate translations, double negatives of the Latin and French are turned into positive expressions. For example:

> nisi quod ea quae praesciuntur non euenire non possunt (5p4.15-16)
> fors que de ce que les chosez qui sont avant seuez ne peuent en nulle maniere estre empechieez que elles n'aviengnent (16-18)
> but that thilke thinges that the prescience woot byforn ne mowen nat unbetyde? (That is to seyn, that thei moten betide) (33-36)

Even if the substitution of "moten" for "mowen" makes the second translation more forceful than the first—which is doubtful—both translations have essentially the same meaning. In the following passage, in addition to clarifying the double negative, the second translation couples "miracle" with "mervayle" in a doublet. Since both words were current in Chaucer's day, the doublet seems to achieve no semantic clarification.

> Non enim dissimile est miraculum nescienti (4p6.99)
> Car ce n'est pas miracle dessemblable, a celui qui ne le scet (111-12)
> Ne it ne is nat an unlik miracle to hem that ne knowen it nat (as who seith, but it is lik a mervayle or miracle to hem that ne knowen it nat) (200-3)

In the following passage, "wot" is substituted for "ne unwot"; "betide" is perhaps more expressive than "be," but "wel" seems to add little to the sentence. Similarly, "hath no necessite" has no apparent advantage over "wanteth necessite." Although the latter two phrases are in fact double translations, with "hath no necessite" reflecting "n'a point de neccessité" and "wanteth necessite" reflecting "necessitate carere," there is still no difference in meaning between the two phrases—or between the two translations.

> cum exstaturum quid esse cognoscit quod idem ex necessitate carere non nesciat (5p6.81-83)
> quant diex cognoist aucune chose ou a estre ou a avenir, la quelle il meismes scet certainement que elle n'a point de neccessité de estre (93-95)

whan that God knoweth any thing to be, he ne unwot not that thilke thing wanteth necessite to be. (This is to sein that whan that God knoweth any thing to betide, he wot wel that it ne hath no necessite to betyde.) (158-62)

In other alternate translations, the second of Chaucer's two translations is simply more idiomatic than the first. For example:

"Manebunt" (3p11.7)
"Elles te demourront ottroiees" (7)
"Thei dwellen graunted to the," quod I. (This to seyn as who seith, "I graunte thi forseide conclusyouns.") (13-15)

In the following passage one sees Chaucer struggling to turn a bit of concise Latin, translated almost word-for-word by Jean, into idiomatic English. In the first translation Chaucer substitutes "wyght" for "si quid" and "riens," which, even if strictly speaking a mistranslation, is perhaps an attempt to give the sentence an idiomatic tone. But if this is the case, Chaucer frustrates the attempt by translating "ex appositis" and "des chosez ajusteez" with the overly literal expansion "that ben put to hym." In the second translation Chaucer preserves the inanimate subject of the Latin and French, although he inserts a "man" — rather than a "wyght" — in a subordinate clause. Having done this, he renders the remainder of the sentence much more idiomatically than he did the first time. Had Chaucer combined the first part of the first translation with the second part of the second translation, he would have produced a sentence more successful than either of his translations.

nam si quid ex appositis luceat (2p5.81)
Car s'il y a riens des chosez ajusteez qui luise (96)
For yif a wyght schyneth with thynges that ben put to hym (as thus, yif thilke thynges schynen with whiche a man is aparayled) (162-64)

One more example of alternate translation will suffice:

Quid autem est quod in alium facere quisque possit, quod sustinere ab alio ipse non possit (2p6.29-30)
Mais quelle chose est ce que chascun puisse faire a autrui que il ne puisse recevoir de autrui, ce meismes en soy (34-35)

> But what thing is it that a man may doon to an other man, that he ne may resceyven the same thyng of other folk in hymself? (Or thus: what may a man don to folk, that folk ne may don hym the same?) (61-66)

Even though Chaucer's two translations have the same meaning, the second translation is clearly more effective than the first. Chaucer eliminates the empty introductory clause of both the Latin and French—"But what thing is it that"—and then substitutes "folk" for "man" as the indirect object. By reorganizing the second half of the sentence so that "folk" rather than "he" is the subject, Chaucer is able to juxtapose the two occurrences of "folk" and repeat "don," the infinitive in the first half of the sentence. He further tightens the sentence by eliminating the two unnecessary occurrences of "other" and—since "folk" is the subject of the second half of the sentence—"of" and "in hymself." In short, Chaucer reduces a rambling sentence of twenty-seven words into a cohesive one of fifteen; by paring out excess words and emphasizing the balance between the two halves, Chaucer is able to reflect the content of the sentence in its structure.

What is striking, then, about the alternate translations is that in every case there are no semantic differences between the two translations. If there were semantic differences, one could argue that the two translations reflect Chaucer's attempt to express the various shades of meaning of his original. Here, however, the variations are essentially stylistic—e.g. the substitution of "man" for "wyght," the replacement of a single word with an alliterating doublet, or the use of more idiomatic language—so that one sees Chaucer exercising his translation and literary skills in order to produce two different ways of saying the same thing. But such stylistic variation is characteristic of the first version of any translation. A translator naturally writes down several possible translations of a given word, clause or sentence. Upon reflection and fuller understanding of the context, a translator who intends to edit his translation into a finished literary product then selects which word or words are most contextually appropriate. Since the alternate translations do nothing to clarify the meaning of

Boece, it is difficult to account for them as being anything other than the marks of the first version of a translation. Indeed, the "as thus" and "Or thus" of the last two passages cited clearly do not introduce glosses for the reader but rather suggest Chaucer the translator's notes to himself. Alternate translations occur neither in Jean de Meung's translation nor in Chaucer's other prose translations. Similar passages do occur in some of Caxton's translations, from which Blake (1969:137) has also concluded that the translations were unrevised: "The repetition of a passage and the variation in the translation of individual words show that Caxton often worked in haste. He did not go over what he had written, or he would have eliminated one of his two versions."[4]

One final apparently insignificant but actually cogent bit of evidence which suggests that *Boece* is unrevised is the absence of a preface to the translation. First, it should be noted that Chaucer's other prose translations have prefaces which identify the audience (the *Astrolabe*), justify the subject matter (the *Parson's Tale*), or apologize for the narrative structure (*Melibee*). One would imagine that Chaucer would have provided a similar explanatory preface for a work as long and important as the *Consolation*. Moreover, *Boece* is the type of work on which, as Green has shown, a medieval writer's livelihood depended. Green (1980:161) notes that

> didatic literature, whether in the form of straight instructional treatises or useful 'ensamples' from the past, was much sought after by the aristocracy of the later middle ages, and ... authors, either by compilation and abridgement of recognized authorities, or by direct translation of them, were likely to attract a more favourable reception from their masters than they were by contributing to the literary tradition of the courtly 'game of love.' ... the writer who wished for recognition and support *as a writer* had to set himself up as a practical and moral mentor to his master.[5]

In this light, one may suppose that Chaucer would have originally undertaken the translation for a patron of the noble class, and if this is the case, one would expect a preface extolling the virtues of the patron and emphasizing the humility of the author. Indeed, Chaucer had a model for just such a preface in Jean de Meung's preface, which itself is largely a copy of William of Aragon's preface to his commentary on the *Consolatio*. It seems highly unlikely, then, that Chaucer would consciously omit a preface to *Boece* when a preface was thus indicated by his own translation procedure, by the literary conventions of the day, and by Jean's made-to-order example.[6]

One might argue that *Boece*, like many medieval translations, was meant only as an aid to a reader working through the original text, and that if it were indeed intended as a gloss on the Latin, it naturally would lack the stylistic polish of a finished translation. Indeed, the "mise en page" of C.U.L. MS Ii.3.21 — one of the best manuscripts of *Boece* and the base manuscript for the editions of Furnivall, Skeat and Fisher — might support such an argument. In the manuscript each "prosa" or "metrum" of the *Consolatio* is followed by the corresponding "prosa" or "metrum" of *Boece*; and the Latin passages are written in a clear, semi-uncial hand, while the English translations are written in a smaller, cursive hand. Moreover, the extensive use of Trevet's commentary in marginal and interlinear glosses in the Latin and English texts, as well as the other commentary material,[7] suggests that whoever had the manuscript made desired a "Summa Consolationis" — a text which had all the aids necessary for a proper understanding of Boethius. There are, however, three problems with this argument. First, the "mise en page" of C.U.L. MS Ii.3.21 testifies only for the desires of its owner, not for the intentions of Chaucer. Second, *Boece* is largely a translation of the French, and so it would seem unlikely that it is intended as a gloss to the Latin. And third, even in those passages which are indebted to the Latin, there are syntactic structures and words which make sense only if one reads Latin; it does an English reader no good to "gloss" "proscriptio" with "proscripcion."[8]

In any event, the fact that Deschamps regarded Chaucer as a "grant translateur" does not prove that *Boece* is a finished literary product, nor does the fact that Lydgate, Shirley and Caxton thought highly of it. Deschamps, of course, is not thinking of *Boece* but of Chaucer's other French "translations," such as the *Book of the Duchess*. And Lydgate's, Shirley's and Caxton's opinions of *Boece*, which were no doubt colored by their opinions of Chaucer in general, reveal nothing about Chaucer's intentions. Neither does the fact that copies of *Boece* circulated during Chaucer's lifetime, as one can infer from *Adam Scriveyn* and the Prologue to the *Legend*, prove that Chaucer was finished with it.[9] The variations in *Troilus* and in the prologues, endlinks and *Canterbury Tales* themselves show that Chaucer continued to revise his work even after the public had access to it. If one cannot find a pattern in the manuscript variation for *Boece*, it may mean only that Chaucer did not revise *Boece* once it had gained general currency, not that he was finished with it when it did. Indeed, in the quotation which prefaces this chapter, Chaucer's countryman Thomas Browne describes how his *Religio Medici* found its way into general currency without revision and without his approval.

If in fact *Boece* is not a finished literary product, most probably it is either a rough draft—i.e. the first version of a translation which Chaucer intended to polish and submit to the public—or a working copy—i.e. a reference tool which Chaucer consulted when incorporating the ideas of the *Consolation* into his poetry, as in *Troilus*, or when preparing a "literary" translation, as *The Former Age*. Of the two, it is more likely to be a rough draft. If Chaucer had desired only a working copy, his facility with French would very likely have allowed him to use Jean's translation as easily as his own. It is true that in the preface to his translation Jean states that he translated the *Consolatio* into French not because Philip IV was unable to read Latin, but because it was easier for him to read French;[10] and it might be argued that although Chaucer, similarly, could read French, it was easier for him to read English. Chaucer's situation, however, was far different from Philip's; Jean was writing to a royal patron, and it is not out of the question that he was flattering Philip by exaggerating the king's knowledge of Latin. Chaucer, on the other hand, was an accomplished courtier and statesman in the courts of Edward III and Richard II, and consequently it is difficult not to think that he was as fluent in French as he was in English. Why he might have left *Boece* unrevised is problematic. Perhaps he simply lost interest in the translation, or perhaps he became more interested in his poems which incorporate the ideas of the *Consolation*; for it was during the 1380s, after the composition of *Boece*, when Chaucer probably wrote the five Boethian balades, *Troilus* and the *Knight's Tale*.

In response to the questions raised at the beginning of this chapter, then, one must first admit that there are no indisputable answers. However, the fact that the very nature of *Boece* suggests that it may be a rough draft perhaps obviates the questions. The lexical and syntactic experimentation and the alternate translations suggest that Chaucer never revised his translation. The very fact that Chaucer indulges himself so thoroughly in lexical experimentation may even imply that he never intended *Boece* for the general public, that he viewed the translation as, in part, a personal exercise for increasing the flexibility and expression of his own language. On the other hand, Green's work indicates that *Boece* is just the sort of composition by means of which a fourteenth-century writer would make his living; this being so, the omission of a preface—in addition to the lack of stylistic polish—compellingly suggests that Chaucer never regarded the translation as complete. Thus, if one cannot definitively answer the questions of why and for whom did Chaucer prepare *Boece*, one can put forth the strong possibility that *Boece*, in its present form, was not intended for the general public.

CHAPTER 6

TOWARDS AN EVALUATION OF CHAUCER AS TRANSLATOR

I am sometimes told that there are people who want a study of literature wholly free from philology; that is, from the love and knowledge of words. Perhaps no such people exist. If they do, they are either crying for the moon or else resolving on a lifetime of persistent and carefully guarded delusion. If we read an old poem with insufficient regard for change in the overtones, and even the dictionary meanings, of words since its date—if, in fact, we are content with whatever effect the words accidentally produce in our modern minds—then of course we do not read the poem the old writer intended. What we get may still be, in our opinion, a poem; but it will be our poem, not his. If we call this *tout court* 'reading' the old poet, we are deceiving ourselves. If we reject as 'mere philology' every attempt to restore for us his real poem, we are safeguarding the deceit. Of course any man is entitled to say he prefers the poems he makes for himself out of his mistranslations to the poems the writers intended. I have no quarrel with him. He need have none with me. Each to his taste. (Lewis, 1967:3)

C. S. Lewis's enthusiastic endorsement of philology provides a good prelude to the conclusion of this study, for this book, has also argued, far less eloquently I fear, for the importance of understanding what the "old writer"—Chaucer—intended. With *Boece*, as with any work of medieval literature, one cannot be content "with whatever effect the words accidentally produce" today. Indeed, the importance of the medieval Latin-English wordlists in the evaluation of a medieval translation is clear, as is the significance of the syntactic differences between Latin, Old French and Middle English. If these lexical and grammatical issues are disregarded, what we get may still be a translation, but it will be our translation, not Chaucer's. Similarly, if the fact that *Boece* is a translation is disregarded, the text we read is then very much of our own making. It has not been the objective of this book to demonstrate—or even to suggest—that *Boece* is one of the masterpieces of English literature. Rather, I have been concerned only with what the "old writer" intended, for it is only after this has been determined that a just evaluation of what he has produced is possible.

This study indicates that Chaucer had two main intentions in *Boece*, the first of which was to stay as close as possible to his source. In order to do this, he employed techniques such as lexical and syntactic derivatives. At the same time, he accommodated his source to English by naturalizing alien syntactic structures, adding particle words to clarify the sense, and employing complex doublets in an attempt to capture the full semantic range of what he was translating. Thus, while there are undeniably awkward and incorrect passages in *Boece*, in the main the translation is accurate and makes for perfectly acceptable Middle English.

Chaucer's other main intention in *Boece*, I have argued, is the manipulation of language. The periphrastic derivatives, lexical and syntactic experimentation, combined translations, double and alternate translations, and many of the doublets suggest an interest in examining how language expresses ideas. That is, the act of composing *Boece* allowed Chaucer the opportunity to explore and expand the means of expression he had used theretofore. I am not here arguing, as Godwin (1804:2.83) did long ago, that Chaucer viewed *Boece* as simply an exercise for the improvement of his composition skills. Rather, I am suggesting that writing *Boece* was in part a way for Chaucer to examine language as language, an area in which, as Tolkien points out in the quotation which begins the first chapter, Chaucer had a pronounced interest. Whether Chaucer subsequently reused any of the words, phrases or structures which he essayed in *Boece* is not to my point (though he did). Once having explored the potential of language—and *Boece*, given its sources and Chaucer's use of them, was perfectly suited to this end—Chaucer's understanding and use of language could not but be significantly altered. Having written *Boece* the way he did, Chaucer's powers of expression were necessarily wider than they had been before. This is not to say, however, that *Boece* has no interest by itself. Indeed, *Boece* is of particular interest, for it not only illustrates one competent medieval translator's technique, but also serves as a background against which to assess Chaucer's use of language in his subsequent compositions. The modes of expression Chaucer uses in *Boece*, because many of them are so distinctive, may in fact prove to be extremely valuable in solving the nagging problem of dating Chaucer's works.[1]

In any event, these two intentions—for a close translation and for the manipulation of language—clearly dominate any interest Chaucer may have had in literary artistry in *Boece*. Moreover, the second objective in particular indicates that *Boece* as we have it was not meant for the general public. At the risk of "crying for the moon," I would venture that the evidence suggests either that *Boece* is a rough draft, or that the "old writer" never intended his translation for circulation.

Throughout this book the term "source" has been used without qualification, and it is to the issue of Chaucer's conception of a source that I now wish to turn. For an examination of what Chaucer understood by a source provides valuable insights into what he understood by translation. On one level, the source of most of Chaucer's lexicon and syntax in *Boece* is Jean's translation,[2] but to stop with this observation alone is to disregard how Chaucer evidently viewed what he was doing. The important and provocative point is that Chaucer draws on the Latin and two commentary traditions as well as the French. All of these works constitute the source which Chaucer translated closely, and so one needs to ask "What relationship did Chaucer perceive between these works? Did one of them have authority over the others?"

In answer to the last question one is intially tempted to say "the Latin," for when Jean abridges or unnecessarily expands upon the Latin, as was discussed in Chapter Four, Chaucer tends to stay close to Boethius. But again this answer obscures the issues, for Chaucer in no way distinguishes or discriminates between his sources in his text;[3] even the occasional "Glosa" and "Textus"—if Chaucer is indeed responsible for them—are ambiguous, for they do not indicate *which* source text is being glossed by *which* gloss tradition. Thus, *Boece* has the appearance of being translated from one, ready-made source. This clearly is not the case, however. Chaucer has in effect created his own source by compiling the Latin and French texts and the two commentaries and by selectively translating from each. That is, the source of Chaucer's close translation never existed except as it is implied by *Boece*. All of the materials he used were, of course, available to any other translator, but the way Chaucer drew from them to create his source was a product of his own invention.

Consequently, an important distinction must be made here between *De Consolatione Philosophiae*, which Boethius wrote and which is the source of modern translations, and the source of *Boece*. The latter reflects a tradition of translation and interpretation which developed in the Middle Ages; the *Consolatio*—what Boethius actually wrote—may be regarded as a fixed text, but the *Consolation*—the tradition which developed from it—contains a variety of disparate expressions of Boethius's ideas. Each of these expressions claims the authority of the original, though in fact many of them, such as Alfred's version, are quite different from what Boethius actually wrote. To put the matter another way, when Boethius wrote *De Consolatione Philosophiae* in the sixth century, he provided only the first chapter, so to speak, for the *Consolation of Philosophy*. Once Boethius laid down his pen, others took up theirs and, by alteration, addition or deletion, continued the book he began. Some, such as the scribes, may have done so unconsciously, while others, such as those who "modernized" the Latin for the vulgate *Consolatio*, may have done so intentionally. Still others, such as Remigius of Auxerre and Nicholas Trevet, in effect contributed to the meaning of the *Consolation* by providing interpretations of it. Jean de Meung incorporated similar interpretations in his translation, which, by its very nature, also contributed to the *Consolation*, since in expressing the received tradition in another language, he, too, supplemented its meaning.

Though *Boece* contains very little which can be attributed solely to Chaucer, Chaucer did in fact contribute a chapter to the *Consolation*; first, he supplemented its meaning by rendering it in another language, and second, he created another version of the *Consolation* by selectively combining various parts of the tradition. Indeed, the version Chaucer created was the basis of Walton's verse translation, which, with its distinctive presentation of its source, is another chapter in the book Boethius began. Moreover, even though Chaucer may have regarded his translation as unfinished, it was read with interest throughout the fifteenth century. A tradition of glosses developed for *Boece*, just as one had for the *Consolatio*, and these glosses not only accompanied Chaucer's text but also occasionally infiltrated it.[4] Furthermore, the many substantive variants in *Boece* manuscripts indicate that scribes and editors had little reluctance to alter the text in front of them. Thus, Chaucer's version of the variable *Consolation* created still more versions.

In short, while any one modern translation of the *Consolatio* is substantively much like another, medieval versions of the *Consolation*, though all were attributed to the author Boethius, could be quite different. As a source text the *Consolation* was fluid, not static, so that both Chaucer and Walton might have said they translated Boethius, though in fact Chaucer also translated Jean and two commentaries, while Walton essentially versified Chaucer. Thus, in the Middle Ages the *Consolation of Philosophy* was an amorphous text and included a variety of disparate expressions of Boethius's ideas. From some of these disparate expressions Chaucer—or any other medieval translator—created what he was translating and transmitted it to his audience:

> But considre wel that I ne ursurpe not to have founden this werk of my labour or of myn engyn. I n'am but a lewd compilator of the labour of olde astrologiens, and have it translatid in myn Englisshe oonly for thy doctrine. And with swerd shal I sleen envie (*Pref. Astr.* 59-64)[5].

In the case of *Boece*, Chaucer compiled his source, in part, from texts in different languages, but both texts were equally valid as expressions of the ideas of the *Consolation*, for "in alle these langages and in many moo han these conclusions ben suffisantly lerned and taught, and yit by diverse reules; right as diverse pathes leden diverse folk the righte way to Rome" (*Pref. Astr.* 36-40). Thus, while one might perhaps not call Chaucer's consultation of *Li Livres* an act of scholarship, Jean's translation was clearly not just a pony for Chaucer. This conception of a source as something which the translator creates is evident in Chaucer's other translations. For instance, in the *Astrolabe* Chaucer blended the treatises of Messahala and John Sacrobosco, in the *Parson's Tale* those of Peraldus and Pennaforte, and in the *Second Nun's Tale* he switched in mid-story from one of the sources he had compiled to the other (see Reames, 1980). Each of these works is regarded as a translation, but for each of them Chaucer himself has in effect created his source. In this regard, it is interesting to note that the "exact sources" of most of Chaucer's translations remain unknown.

The fluidity of a source for Chaucer has important ramifications in the way Chaucer evidently perceived translation. Indeed, although scholars recognize that translations constitute a large part of the Chaucerian canon, as was pointed out in Chapter One, there is not universal agreement as to which of Chaucer's works are in fact translations. Chesterton (1932:122-23) has implied one relevant guideline by suggesting that when Chaucer "was avowedly writing a translation, of a Latin or French original, he thought nothing of putting in chunks of Chaucer which are not in the original at all." But such a claim is inappropriate for

Boece, for there is very little in it which can be attributed solely to Chaucer; indeed, one cannot speak of a "Chaucerian" *Consolation* the way F. Anne Payne (1968) has spoken of an "Alfredian" one. The *Astrolabe*, on the other hand, apparently contains several large chunks of Chaucer (see Lipson, 1983 and Eisner), while the *Romaunt* contains only bits. Yet *Boece*, the *Astrolabe* and the *Romaunt* are all regarded as translations. Moreover, Alceste calls the *Troilus* a translation, though the source of it is as much Chaucer's own invention as Boccaccio's *Il Filostrato*. While Chaucer certainly would have recognized the difference between his techniques in *Boece* and those in *Troilus*, and while the present study has stressed the modern distinction between translation and adaptation, is it possible that on a larger level, given the fluidity of a source text for Chaucer, he would have seen the two works as different expressions of the same process. That is, did translation for Chaucer exist on a continuum? At one end of this continuum one would place a close translation of one text (e.g. the *Romaunt*) and at the other a recreation of a source text (e.g. *Troilus*); in between one could then place those works which draw to varying degrees on different versions of a source text or which contain varying amounts of Chaucer's original contributions. From this perspective, because amorphous sources are given shape by the translator, all the works on such a continuum may be considered products of Chaucer the translator. At present, however, all of these suggestions must remain tentative, for whether it will eventually be possible to define Chaucerian translation, or indeed medieval translation in general, must await further work.

CHAPTER 1 NOTES

1. Two of the more recent studies in this regard are Boitani (1977, especially 165-89) and (1983); of particular interest in the latter are Barry Windeatt's "Chaucer and the *Filostrato*," pp. 163-83 and Boitani's "Style, Iconography and Narrative: the Lesson of the *Teseida*," pp. 185-99. Also see Schless (1974) and Ruggiers (1979). For a study of the occurrence and sources of Biblical quotations in Chaucer's works, see Thompson (1962). Shoaf (1979) considers Chaucer as a "translator" of the past, and Meier (1981:375), in a brief but informative essay, examines how "Chaucer, through Frenchification and Italianization, creates the new poetic voice in English."

2. One of the most commonly cited discussions of the various theories of translation is Steiner (1975); for a more technical discussion, see Catford (1965). Catford (1965:25) identifies three types of translation: "A *free* translation is always *unbounded* — equivalences shunt up and down the rank scale [i.e., in a grammatical or phonological hierarchy], but tend to be at the higher ranks — sometimes between larger units than the sentence. *Word-for-word* translation generally means what it says: i.e., is essentially *rank-bound* at word-rank (but may include some morpheme-morpheme equivalences). *Literal* translation lies between these extremes; it may start, as it were, from a word-for-word translation, but make changes in conformity

with T[arget] L[anguage] grammar (e.g., inserting additional words, changing structures at any rank, etc.); this may make it a group-group or clause-clause translation." Another good discussion is Nida (1975). For the medieval period in particular, see Amos (1920).

3. In addition to the works noted, one might also mention the *Clerk's Tale*, the *Second Nun's Tale*, the *ABC*, the lost translation of *De Contemptu Mundi* and, possibly, the *Equatorie of the Planetis*.

4. Some of the most important studies are Jefferson (1917), Cline (1928), Geissman (1952), Lipson (1983), Eckhardt (1984) and Eisner (forthcoming). I should like to thank Sigmund Eisner for allowing me to see a copy of the latter paper. For a study of Jean's translation, see Crespo (1969).

5. Cf. Ellis (1982:18): "the study of translation in the Middle English period needs to be put on a more systematic footing than it has enjoyed until now." Ellis bases his system on the concept of the "choices" of a medieval translator, while the present study takes more of a grammatical approach.

6. Another recent study is Lawton (1980), who examines how the demands of alliterative verse influenced one medieval translator.

7. John Purvey, as Hudson (1981) has shown, almost certainly did not write the preface in question, but for the sake of convenience I shall call it the "Purvey preface."

8. Epistula LVII, "Ad Pammachium De Optimo Genere Interpretandi," §5. The idea goes back to Horace's *Ars Poetica* 11.131-35 and thence to Cicero's *De Optimo Genere Oratorum* §14.

9. For examples of the various ways in which the idea might be phrased, see Workman (1940:74-76). Jean de Meung, in the preface to his translation of the *Consolatio*, also claims he has followed the Hieronymic principle: "je preisse plainement la sentence de l'aucteur sens trop ensuivre les paroles du latin" (Dedeck-Héry, 1952:168). For a discussion of Jean's preface and medieval notions of word-for-word and sense-for-sense translation, see Cline (1936). Workman (1940:79) suggests that there is inconsistency between Jean's preface and his translation technique—which Cline denies—but notes that in his preface Jean is simply "cultivating prologue manners" and that by "the fifteenth century 'meaning for meaning, not word for word' had become one of the things a French translator might be expected to say no matter how he treated his source."

10. For examples of the latter two, see Ellis (1982:20-30).

NOTES

11. Also see *TC*.1.393-98 and the *Prologue* to the *Second Nun's Tale*, *CT*.VIII.78-84.

12. It should also be pointed out that, given the medieval respect for "auctores," calling a work a translation also lends it a certain authority. Cf. the mention of Petrarch at the beginning of the *Clerk's Tale* and of Lollius in the *Troilus*.

13. John Shirley attributes *Boece* to Chaucer in a prefatory poem in B.M. MS Add. 16165, as does a late fifteenth-century hand in Cambridge Pembroke MS 215. The nine manuscripts mentioned each contain at least half of *Boece*; for complete descriptions see the forthcoming *Variorum Boece*, eds. Jerome Taylor, Alastair J. Minnis and Tim William Machan. For the very short Missouri fragment, see Pace and Voigts (1979). For Bodleian MS Auct. F. 3. 5, which contains a paraphrase of Book One of *Boece*, see Liddell (1896).

14. Cf. Sedgwick (1934:62): "and it apparently was from Jean that he conceived the idea of translating Boethius' *De Consolatione Philosophiae*."

15. Scholars have long been aware that the dates of the *Boece* and the *Troilus* are intimately connected. For a good, balanced discussion, see Fehlauer (1909:31-34), who concludes, "Und so werden wir gut tun, für die Enstehungszeit beider Werke einen grösseren Spielraum zu lassen, für *Troilus* und für *Boethius* 1376-83 oder rund 1380." Most scholars today, however, would not date the *Troilus* as early as 1383.

16. Spurgeon (1925:1.49, 38 and 58). The *Boece* is also mentioned in the will of one John Brinchele, dated July 4, 1420 (Spurgeon, 1925:1.25-26).

17. The Latin manuscript was close to C.U.L. MS Ii.3.21, the value of which was first suggested by Skeat (1900:xxxviii) and seconded by Silk (1930), though Kottler's tempering (1953:153 and 174) of Silk's conclusions—for which see Chapter Four—is important. Chaucer's French manuscript evidently had striking similarities with Besançon MS 434, though in the main it was quite close to B. N. MS fr. 1097 (Dedeck-Héry, 1944). For a full discussion of Chaucer's sources and these manuscripts in particular, see the *Variorum Boece*. The best discussion currently available is Lawler (1984.300-1). For the commentaries mentioned, see Chapter Four.

18. Throughout this study I shall use *Consolation* to refer to the *combined* sources from which Chaucer produced the *Boece*. *Consola-*

tio and *Li Livres*, of course, refer specifically to the Latin and French texts. The reasons for this distinction will become clear in Chapter Six.

CHAPTER 2 NOTES

1. Jeffrey Huntsman (1976:279) notes that "some of the most frustrating puzzles of medieval textual criticism may result from the genuine variants or the simple confusions found in contemporary reference works. If Chaucer 'misused' an English word or 'mistranslated' a Latin one, he may have done so with the reassuring support of a standard dictionary like the *Medulla* at his elbow."

2. The *Ortus* is cited from a facsimile edition which is not paginated. References to the *Promptorium* are to columns, not pages, in the edition.

3. *MED*, s. v. "mere-maiden" sense (a). E.g. "But it was wondir lyk to þe Song of mermaydens of the see ... Though we mermaydens clepe hem here in English ... Men clepe hem sereyns in Fraunce" (*R. Rose* 680). Also sense (b), "*fig*. one who misleads or deceives": "Jerom ... In þe secund prolog ... seiþ: we, hasting to oure countre, schullen passe wiþ a deffe eere to þe dedely soungyis of þe mermaidens" (*Purvey Determ.* 178/272). Also see Pearsall's note (1983) on the pertinent line from the *Nun's Priest's Tale*.

4. See Huntsman's note on p. 842 of his edition of the *Medulla*.

5. The *MED* cites this passage as the earliest occurrence of "foreign" in the sense "not one's own, belonging to someone else" [sense 3.(a)]; this may be the case, but if so, Chaucer (and Jean) has still incorrectly translated the Latin.

6. The only citations of this plural usage in the *MED* are from *Boece*; s. v. "erthe" n. (1) sense 12. From line 20 inclusive until the end of this prose in Robinson's edition, every group of ten lines is counted as if it were a group of five, so that line 320 is numbered 315, line 330 is numbered 320 and so forth. Here and elsewhere, I have supplied the correct line numbers.

7. In the medieval universities "cursus" was used to refer to a "course of study," so that in the universities one might speak of "running through" a text. However, the *OED* does not record "run through" — meaning "to examine, inspect, peruse, treat of, or deal with rapidly" (s. v. sense III.68.a) — until 1449, and it does not record "run by" at all.

8. Ellis (1982) briefly notes several of the techniques isolated in this and the following sections in his discussion of "grammatical relations." However, as the following analysis suggests, I think the techniques are better regarded as aspects of lexical selection.

9. The *Medulla* (401) defines "mollesco" as "inchoatiuum de moleo," while the *Ortus* defines it as "inchoatiuum... to be soft."

10. It is worth noting that the *Ortus* glosses "flagitiosus" as "luxuriosus."

11. In the *Catholicon* (87) one of the definitions of "cursed" is "nefandus."

12. Cf. Blake's observation (1969:142) on Caxton's use of doublets: "But their use in Caxton as in most authors is generally reserved for passages in the high style or for statements which call for particular emphasis. Consequently in his works we find it particularly in his prologues and epilogues, and also at the beginning and end of paragraphs and chapters." For Chaucer's translation of tautological doublets in the *Romaunt*, see Nordahl (1978).

13. "inquam" is supplied from C.U.L. MS Ii.3.21.

14. On other occasions, however, the derivatives Jean and Chaucer use retain the meaning of the Latin, and so the doublets achieve no semantic distinction. For example: "gloriosum" (3p6.15), "glorieus et renomméz" (15) and "glorious and renomed" (25).

15. Robinson punctuates by enclosing "here and undirstand" within parentheses. This punctuation suggests that "here" is a verb paired with "undirstand" in a gloss of "Have now." However, it is more likely that "here" is an adverb, and so I have repunctuated accordingly.

16. "relictus" is supplied from C.U.L. MS Ii.3.21; Bieler's text has "reliquus."

17. I exclude, again, the Missouri fragment and the paraphrase in Bodleian MS Auct. F. 3. 5.

18. Robinson's text reads "nat nat yit," but none of the manuscripts or early editions includes the second "nat," and so its inclusion must be a typographical error.

19. The *OED* records the verb "consider" in the sense "to contemplate" before it records it in the sense "to view"—s. v. senses 1 and 3.

20. Possible exceptions are "ordene" at 3p12.40 and "ryght ordene" at 4p1.41; the French has a preterite participle—"ordenéz (19) and "tres ordenee" (26)—in both instances, while the Latin has "dispositos" (18) and "dispositissima" (19). French verbs, when adopted in Middle English, generally joined the weak conjugations (Brunner,

137

§71), so that one would expect Chaucer to use "ordened," a form which in fact he frequently uses elsewhere. However, "ordene" in these passages is probably an adjective (*OED*, s. v.). Cf. *TC*.1.891-92: "the firste poynt is this / Of noble corage and wel ordayné."

Chaucer's use of native English word-formation patterns for both simple derivatives and neologisms has important implications. Mukařovský (1970:53-54) has noted that "poetic [here in the broader sense of literary] neologisms arise as intentionally esthetic new formations, and their basic features are unexpectedness, unusualness, and uniqueness. Neologisms created for communicative purposes, on the other hand, tend towards common derivation patterns and easy classifiability in a certain lexical category; these are the properties allowing for their general usability." Thus, according to Mukařovský's analysis, Chaucer's neologisms are designed for communication, not aesthetics. This emphasis fits well with Chaucer's overall interest in meaning rather than literary artistry, for which see Chapter Four.

21. Fehlauer (1909:37-38) regards the technique as less intentional than I: "oft gibt er dasselbe Word einfach in englischer Orthographie, sei es, dass es kein entsprechendes Wort im Englischen gab, sei es, dass ihm keins einfiel."

22. "Contrary" and "consequence" are recorded here for the first time, according to the *MED*, and so strictly speaking they are not native derivatives. But even if they are neologisms, the grammatical alterations Chaucer performs are noteworthy.

23. For a discussion of how Chaucer and Jean simplified Boethius's vocabulary, see Burnley (1983:218-19).

24. It is interesting to note that Jean de Meung, in his translation, is responsible for several French neologisms and that when Chaucer borrowed some of these words they became neologisms in English, too. For example: "ajuster" and "imaginable." See Denomy (1954). For an excellent discussion of the ingenuity behind Chaucer's neologisms, see Donner (1984). For a classified list of all the romance neologisms in *Boece*, see Oizumi (1968 and 1969).

25. Fischer very reasonably argues that King Alfred's vocabulary was as suited to the task of translating the *Consolatio* as Chaucer's. But it must be noted that the majority of Alfred's abstract and philosophical words, many of them compounds, had passed out of currency long before Chaucer was born.

26. "plungeux" is supplied from Bes MS 434; Dedeck-Héry's text reads "pleuieus."

27. Robinson's text reads "reflect," which is a typographical error for "refect," found in all of the manuscripts and early printed editions.

28. When discussing Chaucer's derivatives which are also neologisms, Catford's distinction between translation and transference is important. In transference, Catford (1965:48) points out, "there is an *implantation* of S[ource] L[anguage] meanings into the T[arget] L[anguage] text." He observes (1965:46) that in "'real life' transference is not very common. At first sight, it seems as if the use by a translator of an SL lexical item embedded in a TL text is pure transference. Yet reflection shows... that an SL lexical item in these circumstances does not fully retain its SL meaning." Thus, even given the often fluid distinction between French and English in the fourteenth century, the meaning of many of Chaucer's neologisms would have been unclear to his contemporaries.

29. Although Ellis (1982:29) does not use the term calque, this is what he has in mind when he notes that Rolle provides "native equivalents for both elements of compound Latin words, so that the whole translated word exactly duplicates its Latin original." In comparison to Chaucer's calques, the examples Ellis (1982:43, n. 40) cites are quite simplistic: "downren" for "defluet," "manyfaldid" for "multiplicati" and "wele did" for "benefacit." Ellis (1982:30) suggests that Rolle is arguing "for the translation of abstract and compound words in ways that will not be heard again until the sixteenth century." But although no fourteenth or fifteenth-century author may have argued expressly for the use of calques, the evidence of *Boece* and of the fifteenth-century wordlists indicates that calques were in fact used.

30. Fischer (1979:633) thinks that "the fact that Chaucer does not always adapt the same Latin word to English in quite the same way" shows "that many words were not in real use, but probably merely on-the-spot adaptations of the Latin or French word." In support of her argument, she cites "fortunel" and "governailles." But if anything, Chaucer's varying treatment of the same word seems to be further evidence that he was experimenting with words.

31. I arrived at this figure by counting my way through Tatlock's *Concordance*. Verbs or nouns which are recorded in another tense or number are not included, nor are participles which occur in a different usage (e.g. adjectival when the substantival use is limited to *Boece*). Alternate spellings also are not counted. Verbs and nouns which have different tenses and numbers in *Boece* are counted only once, but participles which have different usages (e.g. both adjectival and sub-

stantival) are counted for each usage. If the latter had been counted only once, there would be 503 nonce words in *Boece*.

32. The last two lines of this table were taken from a table in Mersand (1939:54-55). The figures for nonce words in the *Astrolable*, the *Melibee* and the *Parson's Tale* are my own estimates. Mersand counted only romance neologisms and had access to only the beginning of the *MED*, so the total number of neologisms in each work may be slightly different. Cf. Donner (1984:187): "Out of about 2,700 different words that appear in *Boece*, some 200 are new adoptions from French or Latin and more than 150 are new derivations formed on contemporary English patterns." Scheps (1979) has counted 81 nonce words in the *Parson's Tale*, but for the sake of consistency I use my own, clearly high, estimate. Scheps (1979:70) does not consider the *Astrolabe* or *Boece* in his study of Chaucer's nonce words, because they are "close translations" in which it is not "useful or practical to examine frequency of nonce words." As the present discussion makes clear, I do not agree with this assessment.

CHAPTER 3 NOTES

1. The *OED* does not record "rule" in the sense "a principle regulating or determining the form or position of words in a sentence" until 1495 (s. v. "rule" sb. sense II.7.c), but it does record "rule" in the more general sense "a principle regulating practice or procedure" in 1387 (s. v. sense I.3). The semantic leap from the latter sense to the former is short, and in any event the context of "reule" in the *Astrolabe* clearly indicates that Chaucer is using the word in reference to grammar.

2. Open translation is what primarily distinguishes "sense for sense" from "word for word" translation, and so its adoption is of the most profound importance in the history of English translation. A discussion of open translation would figure prominently in any general consideration of late medieval English translation.

The grammatical shibboleths discussed here, it should also be noted, are perhaps not absolutely distinguishable from some of the syntactic derivatives considered later in this chapter. That is, both types of constructions occur in Middle English, and so differentiation between them rests in part on a general sense of what is idiomatic in Middle English and what is not.

NOTES

3. See Trevisa's comments in his letter to Lord Berkeley which prefaces his translation of the *Polychronicon*: "I wote that it is your will for to make this translacion clere and playn to be knowen and vnderstonden. In somme place I shall sette word for worde, and actyf for actyf, and passyf for passyf, arowe right as it stondeth, withoute chaungynge the ordre of wordes. But in somme place I muste chaunge the ordre of wordes, and sette actyf for passyf, and ayenward. And in somme place I must sette a reson for a worde, and telle what it meneth. But for al suche chaungyng, the menyng shal stande and not be chaunged" (cited in Lawler, 1983:268). The original citation is *Cronica Ranulphi Cestrensis Monachi: the book named Prolyconycon* [sic] (Westminster: William Caxton, 1492) iii^v. Although the *Polychronicon* clearly is not Scripture, it does contain numerous citations of the Bible.

4. Dedeck-Héry reads "vertu"; the plural form is supplied from Bes MS 434.

5. "censeo" is supplied from C. U. L. MS Ii.3.21.

6. See Mustanoja (1960:551-64) and Visser (1966: §1105-24). Mustanoja (1960:555) notes, "In the course of ME the appositive participle becomes quite common, possibly supported by the parallel French and Latin usages, although the role of foreign influences is sometimes exaggerated. Wyclif's language is illuminating in this respect. Under Latin influence the Wycliffite translation of the Bible makes extensive use of the appositive participle. In Wyclif's original works the influence of Latin is much less noticeable." The influence of Latin on this usage is evident in *Boece*, for almost all of the appositive verbal adjectives which Chaucer does use match similar structures in the *Consolatio*.

7. See Kerkhof (1982: §888-900). With the example given above compare *CT*.II.617-18: "For as the lomb toward his deeth is broght, / So stant this innocent bifore the kyng." Also see Mustanoja (1960:643-47), who points out that "the innocent" of the first Wycliffite Bible is rendered as "the innocent man" in the revised version.

8. "de li qui est innocent" is supplied from Bes MS 434; Dedeck-Héry's text reads "de toy innocent."

9. "a" is supplied from C.U.L. MS Ii.3.21.

10. Cf. *PF*.18: "it happede me for to behold." For other examples see Kerkhof (1982: §132).

11. Mossé (1952: §178) simply notes that in Middle English the object may occur before the subject, while Jesperson (1949:68-69)

records several examples of the construction throughout the history of English. OSV has perhaps always been a marked structure, intended for stylistic emphasis, and Chaucer's indiscriminate use of the construction is thus stylistically ineffective. Yet the point is that OSV word order does occur in native Middle English writing.

12. The examples are taken from Roscow (1981:20). Roscow (1981:19) suggests that in Chaucer's poetry such "displacement" of the object, as well as other displacements, "normally occurs in subordinate clauses," though in the two examples from *Boece* the object is part of the main clause.

13. Kerkhof (1982: §179) cites this passage and directs the reader to "cause" v.[1] sense 1.d in the *OED*, where there are several examples of "cause" with an infinitive but without an object to serve as the subject of the infinitive. Chaucer's usage of "is covenable" is certainly conditioned by "conuenit," but the medieval usage of "cause" indicates that such a structure was not unknown in Middle English.

14. For a good discussion of how Chaucer's knowledge of French influenced his English, see Donaldson (1981).

15. See Kerkhof (1982: §737) for examples of postposed adjectives and (§738) for examples of plural adjectives. In all but one of the passages he cites—from the *Troilus*—the plural adjectives are also postposed, the normal position for attributive adjectives in Old French. Most of Kerkhof's examples are from prose works—the *Astrolabe* and *Melibee*.

16. Another example of what is possibly a plural adjective is: flagitiosisque ciuibus (1p4.19) / tormenteurs citeiens (21-22) / turmentours citezeens (37). Although neither the *OED* nor the *MED* records "citizen" as an adjective, it seems to be used as such here. Skeat (1900:423), on the other hand, suggests that "the substantives are in apposition."

17. See Roscow (1981:29-33) for examples of the nuances in the structure.

18. For a good discussion of parataxis in English—and of the frequently unacknowledged subtleties of expression which are intrinsic in it—see Mueller (1984). Also see Roscow (1981:132-41).

19. "desine" is supplied from C. U. L. MS Ii.3.21.

20. "de toy" before "tes chetivez" is supplied from Bes MS 434.

21. Cf. the various additions, cuts and rearrangements discussed by Ellis (1982:20-26).

22. See the discussion in the Purvey preface (Forshall and Madden, 1850:1.57): "Also whanne riȝtful construccioun is lettid by relacion, I resolue it openli, thus, where this reesoun, *Dominum formidabunt adversarij ejus*, shulde be Englisshid thus bi the lettre, *the Lord hise aduersaries shulen drede*, I Englishe it thus bi resolucioun, *the aduersaries of the Lord shulen drede him*; and so of othere resons that ben like."

23. Fristedt (1973:39) notes that "the evolution of the *Polychronicon* is strictly that of the Wycliffe Bible, which passed from stark literalness to the First Revision and the Later Revision, frequently via corrections in the manuscripts." Fristedt suggests that Trevisa revised his translation, and that in the later versions the language is increasingly "modernized."

CHAPTER 4 NOTES

1. "puissent" is supplied from Bes MS 434; Dedeck-Héry's text reads "peussent."

2. Souter (1968), s. v. "locus" sense 23: "A part of speech, book, or other composition, section, chapter, passage."

3. Robinson's text, which is based on C.U.L. MS Ii.1.38, does not have "ne" before "loketh." While C.U.L. MS Ii.3.21 does have this "ne," it does not have the "ne" found in Ii.1.38 before "taketh." However, Chaucer is so close to Jean in this passage that I believe he intended both negatives.

4. Robinson isolates the "gloss" from Lady Philosophy's statement by putting quotation marks after the first "knowynge." In general, Robinson is inconsistent in his punctuation of Chaucer's "glosses"— whether they be actual glosses, double translations, or alternate translations, for which see Chapter Five—and this inconsistency is a good indication of the problems involved in interpreting much of *Boece*. That is, is there a Chaucerian "voice" in the text which speaks the glosses? Are they to be ascribed to Boethius the writer? Or are they to be variously ascribed to the Boethian "persona" and to Lady Philosophy?

5. Mark Liddell (1897) contended that many of the glosses are derived from the commentary of the Pseudo-Aquinas, but Kate Peterson (1903) demonstrated that Trevet was the more likely source.

Alastair Minnis, who is working on the commentary tradition for the Variorum *Boece*, has shown that all of the glosses which are not from Jean or Chaucer's original contributions are derived from Trevet or from the so-called Remigian glosses. See Minnis (1981 and 1985).

6. Ellis (1982:28) describes a similar technique: "When translating Biblical allusions or quotations, writers often drew attention to their actual source..." In Ellis's examples, the pertinent phrases are "seyþe holye write" and "as þe gospel berith witnesse."

7. "homme" is supplied from Bes MS 434.

8. Pertinent here is Catford's discussion (1965:94) of "linguistic untranslatability." This occurs when "the functionally relevant features include some which are in fact formal features of the *language* of the SL text. If the TL has no formally corresponding feature, the text, or the item, is (relatively) untranslatable." Skeat (1900:xxiii) comments rather directly on Stewart's claim: "Mr. Stewart also gives some instances in which Chaucer 'actually reproduces the original Latin metre;' but they are imperfect and unintended."

9. Cited by Skeat (1900:xxiii). The punctuation and line arrangement are Skeat's, but the orthography is that of Robinson's edition.

10. "habet" is supplied from C.U.L. MS Ii.3.21.

11. See her articles "Chaucer's Prose Rhythms" (1950) and "The Art of Chaucer's Prose" (1966). The latter presents the more developed treatment of her theory. She records three types of "cursus"—'xx'x, 'xx 'xx and 'xx'x'x—and notes that there "were numerous variations, depending on the permissable divisions between words (this applied especially to Latin *cursus*), the incidence of secondary stress, and the possibility of introducing extra unstressed syllables—a latitude much favoured in England by the tradition of native metrics" (156). It is the last qualification—the admission of extra unstressed syllables—which seriously undermines her theory. By nature, English syllables alternate between stressed and unstressed. Thus, although there certainly is intentional, cadenced prose in English, once one admits extra unstressed syllables, it is not difficult to find in any English work clauses or sentences which may be said to demonstrate "cursus." For instance, to take examples from this footnote, "demonstrate 'cursus'" illustrates the pattern 'xx'x, "extra unstressed syllables" illustrates—with admission of an extra secondary stress for "-a"—'xx'xx, and "the tradition of native metrics" illustrates 'xx'x'x.

12. Elliott (1974:167) suggests that in "his handling of dialogue between Boethius and the Lady Philosophy, Chaucer achieves for the

most part an easy, colloquial verisimilitude." This is perhaps an exaggeration, however, for the dialogue is frequently very stilted, and many of the colloquial phrases which Elliott cites can be traced to the French. For example: "Ita est" (3p11.21) / "Je l'otroi," dis je (21) / "I graunte it," quod I (43).

It should also be noted that Chaucer, unlike Jean, regularly translates Lady Philosophy's first person plural pronoun with a singular. Given Chaucer's other stylistic techniques, this change probably signifies nothing more than Chaucer's desire to adapt the Latin idiom to the English, where the plural pronoun has a significance it lacks in Latin.

While acknowledging the idiomatic and grammatical differences between Old French and Middle English, Eckhardt (1984:52) suggests that the greater number of first person singular pronouns in the *Romaunt*, in comparison to the plural pronouns or unexpressed subjects in the *Roman*, is a conscious stylistic technique which gives the English translation a "more personal" tone and heightens "the narrator's presence in the poem."

CHAPTER 5 NOTES

1. The quotation is from Browne's preface to the revised edition of *Religio Medici*, pp. 59-60 in Patrides's edition.

2. Cf. Ellis's discussion (1982:26-27) of how medieval translators may gloss "difficult and technical words."

3. The romance neologisms were counted from the lists in the back of Mersand (1939). Only the first occurrence of each word is noted. In 4p6 "mutable" and "muable" occur as variants of each other. Mersand counts both as neologisms, but since one clearly must be a scribal error, they are considered as only one word for the purposes of the chart.

4. Blake regards alternate translations as aspects of Caxton's style as a translator—that is, Blake believes Caxton was not conscientious enough to remove such passages. The absence of alternate translations in Chaucer's other translations makes the passages in *Boece* anomalies.

5. Green continues: "Some authors, such as Chaucer and to a lesser extent Gower, managed to effect a successful compromise between the two roles [of love poet and moral mentor], perhaps in part because in late fourteenth-century England the court poet's position was still ill-defined; the professional minstrel lay in the recent past, the

adviser to princes was yet to emerge completely." Of course, that Chaucer was able to play both roles does not alter the fact that *Boece* is the work of Chaucer the moral mentor, not Chaucer the love poet.

6. It should be noted that there is no reason to believe that Chaucer did write a preface but that it somehow was eliminated in all the extant manuscripts.

7. The manuscript begins with an alphabetized list of "topoi" in the *Consolatio* and, after the alternation of Latin and English texts, concludes with William of Aragon's commentary and a summary of the argument of each "prosa" and "metrum." Samuels (1983) has suggested that this manuscript is one of three which most closely preserve Chaucer's own spelling. But even given this added authority, the manuscript's arrangement still does not necessarily reveal anything about Chaucer's intentions in *Boece*.

8. It is worthwhile to recall here that in C.U.L. MS Ii.3.21 Chaucer's *The Former Age* is inserted after 2m5. The scribe prefaces the poem with "Chawcer vpon this fyfte metur of the second book," and indeed much of the first third of the poem is based on 2m5 of the *Consolatio*. *The Former Age* is followed by *Fortune*, after which the alternation between Latin "prosa" or "metrum" and English translation resumes without interruption. Although *Fortune* is clearly indebted to the *Consolatio*, the resemblances, as Jefferson (1917:58) points out, "are not verbal. They, rather, are conclusions which would result from a thoughtful reading of that work." Indeed, even *The Former Age* cannot be considered a true translation, since half of the "metrum" is not reflected in the poem. Thus, although it is tempting to speculate that Chaucer intended ultimately to polish the prose of the "prosae" and versify the "metra," there is insufficient evidence to do so. Chaucer's poems would have to be much closer to the original, such as Walton's translations are, if he intended them as translations. It is very likely only a coincidence that the texts of both Boethian poems in Ii.3.21 are authoritative within their respective textual traditions, for the poems were almost certainly inserted by a scribe, an editor or the patron of the manuscript.

Lowes (1917) suggested long ago that Chaucer's heavy debt to Jean de Meung clearly accounts for the fact that all the "metra" are rendered in prose. Eckhardt (1983:30), however, dismisses Lowes's argument by saying that it implies Chaucer was "bound to follow the form of the French rather than the Latin one." This is to misinterpret the evidence, however, for while Chaucer was not "bound" to follow the French, the fact of the matter is he did. Eckhardt (1983:31) observes that the tradition of "prosimetrum" in the Middle Ages did not compel Chaucer to use prose and suggests that he did so in *Boece* and in other prose works because he wanted the speakers to be guileless and the substance transparent; in essence, this is a reworking of an old argument. Cf. Chambers (1932:cxi): "Chaucer gave his life to verse, but comforted himself, when death drew near, by reflecting on the moral virtue of his prose." Lowes's argument still strikes me as the most satisfying.

9. There are several ways to read *Adam Scriveyn*, none of which disproves the thesis of this chapter. First, if Adam did prepare, prior to the composition of the poem, copies of *Boece* for circulation, they may have been for Chaucer's close friends who would have been aware that the translation was unrevised—just as Browne's close friends were aware that *Religio Medici* was not, in its first version, intended as a finished literary product. Second, even if *Adam* implies that the scribe had prepared copies of *Boece* for general circulation, he may have done so only because Chaucer, due to his involvement in other literary projects, did not intend to revise the translation. And third, it is possible that when Chaucer admonishes Adam to "wryte more trewe" after his "makyng," Chaucer is referring to defective copies of works other than *Troilus* or *Boece*, copies which Adam had produced and which Chaucer had seen. In this vein, when Chaucer observes that if ever it befalls Adam to "wryten newe" *Boece* or *Troilus*, he does not intend "newe" in the sense "again" but in the sense "anew," so that the first two lines of the poem might be translated: "Adam scriveyn, if ever you happen to write *Boece* or *Troilus* anew"—i.e. whenever you make copies of them. The *OED* groups the senses "anew" and "again" under one definition (s. v. "new" adv. sense 2.a), but the senses are distinct. For an example of Chaucer using the adverb "newe" in the sense "anew" or "in a new way," see *CT*.IV.377-78: "this mayde bright of hewe / Fro foot to heed they clothed han al newe." Earlier in this stanza it is noted that "no thyng of hir olde geere / She sholde brynge into his hous" (372-73), so that it is clear Walter's "wommen" are dressing Griselde in a new way.

10. "Ja soit ce que tu entendes bien le latin, mais toutevois est de moult plus legiers a entendre le françois que le latin" (Dedeck-Héry, 1952:168).

CHAPTER 6 NOTES

1. Koch (1922) attempted as much, though his evidence is insufficient and his conclusions unsubstantiated.

2. Cf. Lawler (1984:300): "no one who has ever studied the matter has doubted that Chaucer made constant use of Jean de Meun." The precise way in which Chaucer approached his sources—e.g. whether he looked at the Latin before the French or vice versa—is not pertinent here, though it is clear that Chaucer had relatively complete copies of both texts in front of him.

3. Cf. Nicholas Love's practice in *The Mirrour of the Blessed Lyf of Jesu Christ*. Ellis (1982:22) notes "the regular indications Love gives his readers of the cuts he is making to his original, including reference even to the chapter numbers of the cut material in the original.... Likewise, he tells us, he will indicate any elaborations to the matter of his original by means of a marginal 'N,' showing where his contribution begins, and a marginal 'B,' for Bonaventura, where the original resumes...."

4. For a discussion of the glosses in the *Boece* manuscripts, see Machan (1986).

5. On the role of "compilators," see Minnis (1979).

BIBLIOGRAPHY

Amos, Flora Ross 1920. *Early Theories of Translation*. New York: Columbia University Press.
Anderson, George 1950. "Old and Middle English Literature from the Beginnings to 1485." In *A History of English Literature*. Ed. Hardin Craig. New York: Oxford University Press, pp. 3-172.
Baum, Paull F. 1946. "Chaucer's Metrical Prose." *JEGP* 45:38-42.
Bieler, Ludovicus, ed. 1957. *Philosophiae Consolatio*. Corpus Christianorum, Series Latina XCIV. Turnholtus: Typographi Brepols.
Blake, N. F. 1969. *Caxton and His World*. New York: London House and Maxwell.
Boitani, Piero, ed. 1983. *Chaucer and the Italian Trecento*. Cambridge: Cambridge University Press.
———— 1977. *Chaucer and Boccaccio*. Medium Ævum Monographs, New Series VIII. Oxford: Society for the Study of Mediæval Languages and Literature.
Brewer, D. S. 1953. *Chaucer*. London: Longmans, Green and Company.
ten Brink, Bernhard 1870. *Chaucer Studien*. Münster: Adolph Russel's Verlag.
Browne, Sir Thomas 1977. *The Major Works*. Ed. C. A. Patrides. London: Penguin Books Ltd.

Brunner, Karl 1963. *An Outline of Middle English Grammar.* Trans. G. K. W. Johnstone. Oxford: Basil Blackwood.

Burnley, David 1983. *A Guide to Chaucer's Language.* London: The MacMillan Press Ltd.

Bynon, Theodora 1977. *Historical Linguistics.* Cambridge: Cambridge University Press.

Cappelli, Adriano 1960. *Dizionario di Abbreviature Latine ed Italiane.* 6th ed. Milan: Ulrico Hoepli.

Catford, J. C. 1965. *A Linguistic Theory of Translation.* London: Oxford University Press.

Catholicon Anglicum 1881. Ed. Sidney J. H. Herrtage. E.E.T.S. O. S. 75. London: N. Trübner and Co.

Chambers, R. W. 1932. *On the Continuity of English Prose.* E.E.T.S. O. S. 191a. Rpt. London: Oxford University Press, 1966.

Chesterton, G. K. 1932. *Chaucer.* 1949; Rpt. London: Faber and Faber Ltd.

Chute, Marchette 1946. *Geoffrey Chaucer of England.* New York: E. P. Dutton and Co.

Cline, James M. 1936. "Chaucer and Jean de Meun: *De Consolatione Philosophiae.*" *ELH* 3:170-81.

——— 1928. "A Study in the Prose of Chaucer's Boethius." Diss. Princeton University.

Courcelle, Pierre 1967. *La Consolation de Philosophie dans la tradition littéraire.* Paris: Études Augustiniennes.

Cowling, George H. 1927. *Chaucer.* London: Methuen and Co., Ltd.

Crespo, Roberto 1969. "Jean de Meun Traduttore della 'Consolatio Philosophiae' de Boezio." *Atti della Accademia delle Scienze di Torino* 103:71-170.

Dedeck-Héry, V. L. 1952. "Boethius' *De Consolatio* by Jean de Meun." *Mediaeval Studies* 14:165-275.

——— 1944. "Le Boèce de Chaucer et les manuscrits français de la *Consolatio* de J. de Meun." *PMLA* 59:18-25.

——— 1940. "The Manuscripts of the Translation of Boethius' *Consolatio* by Jean de Meung." *Speculum* 15:432-43.

——— 1937. "Jean de Meun et Chaucer, traducteurs de la Consolation de Boèce." *PMLA* 52:967-91.

Denomy, Alex J. 1954. "The Vocabulary of Jean de Meun's Translation of Boethius." *Mediaeval Studies* 16:19-34.

Donaldson, E. Talbot 1981. "Gallic Flies in Chaucer's English Word Web." In *New Perspectives in Chaucer Criticism.* Ed. Donald M. Rose. Norman: Pilgrim Books Inc., pp. 193-202.

Donner, Morton 1984. "Derived Words in Chaucer's *Boece*: the Translator as Wordsmith." *Chaucer Review* 18:187-203.
Eckhardt, Caroline D. 1984. "The Art of Translation in *The Romaunt of the Rose.*" *Studies in the Age of Chaucer* 6:41-63.
——— 1983. "The Medieval *Prosimetrum* (from Boethius to *Boece*)." *Genre* 16:21-38.
Eisner, Sigmund "Chaucer's *Treatise on the Astrolabe* as Technical Writing: A Primarily Medieval View." Forthcoming, *Chaucer Review*.
Elliott, Ralph W. V. 1974. *Chaucer's English*. London: André Deutsch.
Ellis, R. 1982. "The Choices of the Translator in the Late Middle English Period." In *The Medieval Mystical Tradition in England*. Ed. Marion Glasscoe. Exeter: Short Run Press Ltd., pp. 18-46.
Fehlauer, Friedrich 1909. *Die englischen Übersetzungen von Boethius' 'De Consolatione Philosophiae.'* Berlin: Emil Felber.
Fischer, Olga 1979. "A Comparative Study of philosophical Terms in the Alfredian and Chaucerian Boethius." *Neophilologus* 63: 622-39.
Fisher, John H. 1977. *The Complete Poetry and Prose of Geoffrey Chaucer*. New York: Holt, Rinehart and Winston.
Forshall, Josiah and Frederic Madden 1850. *The Holy Bible*. Oxford: Oxford University Press.
French, Robert 1947. *A Chaucer Handbook*. New York: F. S. Crofts and Co.
Fristedt, Sven L. 1953, 1969, 1973. *The Wycliffe Bible*. Stockholm: Bröderna Lagerström Boktryckare and Amlqvist and Wiksell.
Gardner, John 1977. *The Poetry of Chaucer*. Carbondale: Southern Illinois University Press.
Geissman, Erwin W. 1952. "The Style and Technique of Chaucer's Translations from French." Diss. Yale University.
Godefroy, Frédéric 1883-1902. *Dictionnaire de l'ancienne langue français*. Paris: F. Vieweg.
Godwin, William 1804. *Life of Chaucer*. 2nd ed. London: Richard Phillips.
Green, Richard Firth 1980. *Poets and Princepleasers*. Toronto: University of Toronto Press.
Grose, M. W. 1967. *Chaucer*. London: Evans Brothers Ltd.
Hudson, Anne 1981. "John Purvey: A Reconsideration of the Evidence for his Life and Writings." *Viator* 12:355-80.

Huntsman, Jeffrey 1976. "Caveat Editor: Chaucer and Medieval English Dictionaries." *Modern Philology* 73:276-79.

Jefferson, B. L. 1917. *Chaucer and the Consolation of Philosophy of Boethius*. Rpt. New York: Gordian Press, 1968.

Jesperson, Otto 1949. *A Modern English Grammar On Historical Principles*. Vol. 7. Ed. Niels Haislund. Rpt. London: George Allen and Unwin Ltd., 1961.

Kerkhof, J. 1982. *Studies in the Language of Geoffrey Chaucer*. 2nd ed. Leiden: E. J. Brill.

Koch, John 1922. "Chaucers Boethiusübersetzung: Ein Beitrag zur Bestimmung der Chronologie seiner Werke." *Anglia* 46:1-51.

Kottler, Barnet 1955. "The Vulgate Tradition of the *Consolatio Philosophiae* in the Fourteenth Century." *Mediaeval Studies* 17:209-14.

——— 1953. "Chaucer's *Boece* and the Late Medieval Textual Tradition of the *Consolatio Philosophiae*." Diss. Yale University.

Krapp, George Philip 1915. *The Rise of English Literary Prose*. Rpt. New York: Frederick Ungar, 1963.

Lawler, Traugott 1984. "Chaucer." In *Middle English Prose*. Ed. A. S. G. Edwards. New Brunswick: Rutgers University Press, pp. 291-314.

——— 1983. "On the Properties of John Trevisa's Major Translations." *Viator* 14:266-88.

Lawton, D. A. 1980. "*The Destruction of Troy* as Translation from Latin Prose: Aspects of Form and Style." *Studia Neophilologica*, 52:259-70.

Lewis, Charlton T. and Charles Short 1879. *A Latin Dictionary*. Oxford: Oxford University Press.

Lewis, C. S. 1967. *Studies in Words*. 2nd ed. Cambridge: Cambridge University Press.

Liddell, Mark 1898. Prefatory note to *Boece*. In *The Works of Geoffrey Chaucer*. Ed. Alfred W. Pollard *et al*. Rpt. London: Macmillan and Co., 1953.

——— 1897. Untitled note. *The Nation* 64 no. 1651:124-25. (Feb. 18)

——— 1896. "Chaucer's Boethius Translation." *Academy*, 49 no. 1244:199-200. (March 7)

——— 1895. "Chaucer's Translation of Boece's 'Boke of Comfort.'" *Academy*, 48 no. 1220:227. (Sept. 21)

Lipson, Carol 1983. "I N'am But a Lewd Compilator: Chaucer's *Treatise on the Astrolabe* as Translation." *Neuphilologische Mitteilungen* 84:192-200.

Lounsbury, Thomas R. 1892. *Studies in Chaucer*. Rpt. New York: Russell and Russell Inc., 1962.

Lowes, J. L. 1917. "Chaucer's *Boethius* and Jean de Meun." *Romanic Review* 8:383-99.

Machan, Tim William 1986. "Glosses in the Manuscripts of Chaucer's *Boece*." In *The Medieval Boethius: Studies in the Vernacular Translations of 'De Consolatione Philosophiae.'* Ed. Alastair J. Minnis. Boydell and Brewer.

——— 1984. *"forlynen*: A Ghost Word Rematerializes." *N&Q* n. s. 31:22-24.

Meier, Hans H. 1981. "Middle English Styles in Translation; the Case of Chaucer and Charles." In *So Meny Poeple Longages and Tonges*. Ed. Michael Benskin and M. L. Samuels. Edinburgh: Middle English Dialect Project, pp. 367-76.

Mersand, Joseph 1939. *Chaucer's Romance Vocabulary*. New York: The Comet Press.

Middle English Dictionary 1956-. Ed. Hans Kurath and Sherman M. Kuhn. Ann Arbor: University of Michigan Press.

Minnis, Alastair J. 1986 "'Glossing is a glorious thing': Chaucer at Work on the *Boece*." In *The Medieval Boethius: Studies in the Vernacular Translations of 'De Consolatione Philosophiae.'* Ed. Alastair J. Minnis. Boydell and Brewer.

——— 1981. "Aspects of the Medieval French and English Traditions of Boethius' *De consolatione philosophiae*." In *Boethius: His Life, Thought and Influence*. Ed. M. T. Gibson. Oxford: Basil Blackwood, pp. 312-61.

——— 1979. "Late-Medieval Discussions of *Compilatio* and the Role of the *Compilator*." *Beiträge zur Geschichte der Deutschen Sprache Literatur* 101:385-421.

Mossé, Ferdinand 1952. *A Handbook of Middle English*. Trans. James A. Walker. Baltimore: The Johns Hopkins Press.

Mueller, Janel M. 1984. *The Native Tongue and the Word*. Chicago: University of Chicago Press.

Mukařovský, Jan 1970. "Standard Language and Poetic Language." In *Linguistics and Literary Style*. Ed. Donald C. Freeman. New York: Holt, Rinehart and Winston Inc., pp. 40-56. Originally printed in *A Prague School Reader on Esthetics, Literary Structure, and Style*. Ed. and trans. Paul L. Garvin. Georgetown University Press, 1964, pp. 17-30.

Mustanoja, T. F. 1960. *A Middle English Syntax*. Helsinki: Société Néophilologique de Helsinki.

Nida, Eugene A. 1975. "Science of Translation." In *Language Structure and Translation, Essays by Eugene A. Nida*. Ed. Anwar S. Dil. Stanford: Stanford University Press, pp. 79-101.

Nordahl, Helge 1978. "Ars fidi interpretis (un aspect rhétorique de l'art de Chaucer dans sa traduction du Roman de la Rose)." *Archivum Linguisticum* 9:24-31.

Oizumi, Akio 1968, 1969. "The Romance Vocabulary of Chaucer's Translation of Boethius's *De Consolatione Philosophiae*." Doshisha University, *Jimbungaku*, Studies in Humanities 108:57-78 and 109:64-95.

Ortus Vocabulorum 1968. Ed. R. C. Alston. Menston: The Scolar Press Ltd.

Oxford English Dictionary 1884-1928. Ed. Sir J. A. H. Murray *et al.* Oxford: Oxford University Press.

Pace, George B. and Linda Voigts 1979. "A *Boece* Fragment." *Studies in the Age of Chaucer* 1:143-50.

Patch, Howard 1935. *The Tradition of Boethius*. Rpt. New York: Russell and Russell Inc., 1970.

Payne, F. Anne 1968. *King Alfred and Boethius*. Madison: University of Wisconsin Press.

Pearsall, Derek 1983. *The Nun's Priest's Tale*. Vol. 2 Part 9 of *A Variorum Edition of the Works of Geoffrey Chaucer*. Ed. Paul G. Ruggiers. Norman: University of Oklahoma Press.

"Pepys MS 2002[1] *Medulla Grammatice*: An Edition." Ed. Jeffrey Huntsman. Diss. University of Texas-Austin, 1973.

Peterson, Kate O. 1903. "Chaucer and Trevet." *PMLA* 18:173-93.

The Promptorium Parvulorum 1908. Ed. A. L. Mayhew. E.E.T.S. E. S. 102. London: N. Trübner and Co.

Reames, Sherry L. 1980. "The Cecilia Legend as Chaucer Inherited It and Retold It: the Disappearance of an Augustinian Ideal." *Speculum* 55:38-57.

Robinson, F. N. 1957. *The Works of Geoffrey Chaucer*. 2nd ed. Boston: Houghton Mifflin Co.

Root, Robert K. 1934. *The Poetry of Chaucer*. Rev. ed. Rpt. Gloucester: Peter Smith, 1957.

Roscow, Gregory 1981. *Syntax and Style in Chaucer's Poetry*. Cambridge: D. S. Brewer.

Ruggiers, Paul G. 1979. "The Italian Influence on Chaucer." In *Companion to Chaucer Studies*. Rev. ed. Ed. Beryl Rowland. New York: Oxford University Press, pp. 160-84.

Saintsbury, George 1907. "Chaucer." In *The End of the Middle Ages*. Vol. 2 of *The Cambridge History of English Literature*. Ed. A. W. Ward and A. P. Waller. New York: G. P. Putnam's Sons, pp. 179-224.

Samuels, M. L. 1983. "Chaucer's Spelling." In *Middle English Studies*. Ed. Douglas Gray and E. G. Stanley. Oxford: Oxford University Press, pp. 17-37.

Scheps, Walter 1979. "Chaucer's Use of Nonce Words, Primarily in the *Canterbury Tales*." *Neuphilologische Mitteilungen* 80:69-77.

Schlauch, Margaret 1966. "The Art of Chaucer's Prose." In *Chaucer and Chaucerians*. Ed. D. S. Brewer. London: Thomas Nelson and Sons Ltd., pp. 140-63.

―――― 1950. "Chaucer's Prose Rhythms." *PMLA* 65:568-89.

Schless, Howard 1974. "Transformations: Chaucer's Use of Italian." In *Geoffrey Chaucer*. Ed. D. S. Brewer. London: G. Bell and Sons Ltd., pp. 184-223.

Sedgwick, Henry Dwight 1934. *Dan Chaucer*. New York: The Bobbs-Merrill Co.

Shoaf, R. A. 1979. "Notes Towards Chaucer's Poetics of Translation." *Studies in the Age of Chaucer* 1:55-66.

Silk, Edmund T. 1930. "Cambridge Ms. Ii.3.21 and the Relation of Chaucer's *Boece* to Trivet and Jean de Meung." Diss. Yale University.

Skeat, W. W. 1900. *Boethius and Troilus*. Vol. 2 of *The Complete Works of Geoffrey Chaucer*. 2nd ed. Oxford: Oxford University Press.

Souter, A. *et al.* 1968. *Oxford Latin Dictionary*. Oxford: Oxford University Press.

Spurgeon, Caroline F. E. 1925. *Five Hundred Years of Chaucer Criticism and Allusion, 1357-1900*. 2nd ed. Rpt. New York: Russell and Russell Inc., 1961.

Steiner, George 1975. *After Babel: Aspects of Language and Translation*. London: Oxford University Press.

Stewart, H. F. 1891. *Boethius*. Rpt. New York: Franklin, 1974.

Tatlock, J. S. P. and Arthur G. Kennedy 1927. *A Concordance to the Complete Works of Geoffrey Chaucer*. Rpt. Gloucester: Peter Smith, 1963.

Thompson, W. Meredith 1962. "Chaucer's Translation of the Bible." In *English and Medieval Studies*. Ed. Norman Davis and C. L. Wrenn. London: Allen and Unwin, pp. 183-99.

Töbler, Adolf and Erhard Lommatzsch 1925-. *Altfranzösisches Wörterbuch*. Berlin: Weidmannsche Buchhandlung.

Tolkien, J. R. R. 1934. "Chaucer as a Philologist: *The Reeve's Tale*." *Transactions of the Philological Society*, pp. 1-70.

Trevet, Nicholas. *Exposicio Fratris Nicolai Trevethi Anglici Ordinis Predicatorum super Boecio De Consolacione*. Ed. E. T. Silk. Unpublished.

Visser, F. Th. 1963, 1966, 1973. *An Historical Syntax of the English Language*. Leiden: E. J. Brill.

Workman, Samuel K. 1940. *Fifteenth Century Translation as an Influence on English Prose*. Princeton: Princeton University Press.

Index of Lines

Individual Words:
   15-18
1p1.68
1p4.251-52
1m5.44
1p6.84
2p3.59-60
3m2.5
3p5.65
4m2.17
4m3.17
4p6.36
5p1.77
5p3.102
5p4.21-22
5p4.165-66

Calques: 18-20
1p4.102
2p1.78-79
2p2.23
2m7.25
2p8.25
3p1.2
3m9.38
3p10.64
4m3.43
4m3.45

4m5.7-8
4p6.2
4p6.107-108
4p6.224
5p1.45
5p1.77
5p6.295

Idioms: 21-23
1p4.115
1p4.146
1p4.205
2p4.79-80
2p4.117-18
2p4.135
2p5.24
2p6.110
3p1.43-44
3p7.20-21
4p4.291
5p1.29-30

Lexical Errors: 24-26
1p1.19-21
1p4.218
2p4.48
2p7.48
2p7.109-12

3p2.84
3p11.68-70
3p11.189
4p4.16
4p6.368

Periphrases 27-32
1p1.19
1p4.50-51
1p4.242-43
1p4.260-61
1m5.49
1p5.76
1p6.98-99
2p2.7-8
2p3.61-62
2p3.82
2p5.18-19
2p6.47-48
2m8.6-7
3p4.9
3p5.16-17
3m5.7
3p6.11
3p9.17-18
3p10.66-67
3p11.28-29
3p11.34-35

INDEX OF LINES

3p11.71
3p11.217-18
4m1.18
4m1.34
4p2.144-45
4p2.229-30
4m3.8
4p4.56-57
4p4.62-63
4p4.124-25
4p6.18
4p6.277-78
5p3.60-61
5p4.86

Combined
   Translation—
   Lexical: 33-34
1p3.63-64
1p4.312
1m5.7-8
2p1.39-40
3p2.43
3p2.88
3m2.1-2
3m2.36-37
3p5.7-8
3p5.45
3p10.94-95
4p2.1
5m3.16-17

Doublets: 35-46
1p1.25-26
1p1.26
1p1.28
1p1.53
1p1.53-54
1p1.66
1p1.78-79

1p3.1
1p3.16-17
1p3.45
1p3.48-49
1p3.75
1p4.8
1p4.19-20
1p4.34-35
1p4.47
1p4.62
1p4.70
1p4.87-88
1p4.99-101
1p4.118-19
1p4.244
1p4.264-65
1m5.43
1m5.44
1p5.40
1p6.18-19
1p6.82
2p1.57
2p1.67
2m2.12
2m3.22-23
2p4.60-61
2p5.13-14
2p5.82-83
2p5.185-86
2m5.19
2p6.87
2p7.20-21
2p7.36-37
2p7.61-62
2p7.86-87
2p7.119-20
2p7.134-35
2p8.42
3p2.39-41
3p2.63

3p2.78-79
3p3.22
3p4.45-46
3p4.91
3m5.5-6
3p6.4
3p7.12
3p8.53-54
3p8.60
3p9.18
3p9.56-57
3p10.108
3p10.110-11
3p11.227-28
4m1.25
4p2.47-48
4p2.57-58
4m2.14
4p4.235-36
4p5.30
4p6.20-21
4p6.64-65
4p6.117
5p1.39-40
5p4.94
5m4.27
5p5.53-54
5p6.181

Lexical and
   Periphrastic
   Derivatives: 46-49
1p4.274
1p4.275-76
2m4.2
2p7.27
2p7.72-73
3p3.19-20
3p3.25-26
3p5.3

INDEX OF LINES

3p5.25
3p6.25 (137 n)
3m8.1
3p9.103
3p9.114-15
3p10.203
3p10.220-21
3p12.40 (137 n)
4p1.41 (137 n)
4p2.54
4p2.136
4p3.82
4p4.114
4p4.239-40
4p4.273
4p6.28
4p6.73-74
4p6.265
4p6.283
4p7.104
5p2.34
5p4.122
5p4.155
5p4.156
5p6.154

Neologisms: 50-53
1p3.19-20
1p3.80-81
1p4.99
1p4.243
3m1.8
3p9.17-18
3p11.64
4p4.280
4p6.140
4p6.374
5p1.95
5p3.200-201
5p4.211

5p6.56-58
5p6.69
5p6.295

Ablative Absolutes:
 65-68
1p3.1-2
1p3.26-27
1p3.41-42
1p4.62-64
1p6.47
1p6.100-101
2p2.32
2p5.86-87
2p7.116-19
3p1.36-38
3m9.41-42
4p2.26
4p2.170-71
5p3.150-51
5p3.203-206

Participles: 68-72
1p3.8-10
1p4.11-12
1p4.25
1p4.56-57
1p4.97-98
2m1.7-8
2m2.14-15
2m4.10-11
3p1.28-29
3p2.32
3p9.197-98
3p10.4
3p11.156
4p2.176-77
4p2.265

Adjectives: 71
1p3.18-19

1m4.13-14
1p4.231-32

Impersonal Verbs:
 72-74
2p4.156
3p9.78
3p10.104-105
3p10.121-22
3p10.140-41
3p10.240-41
3p10.248
3p11.44
4p2.7
4p4.228
4p6.37

Syntactic Derivatives:
 74-78
1p4.37 (142 n)
2p3.25-26
2p5.54-55
3p11.18
3p11.107-108
3m11.9-12
3p12.22-24
4p2.40
4p3.48-49
4p6.364-65
4m6.19
5p2.43-45
5p6.9-10
5p6.188-90

Conjunctions,
 Additions of:
 79-82
1p1.17-19
1p4.179-81
2p1.108-11

INDEX OF LINES

2p8.32-39
2p8.45-48
3p5.60-64
3m5.8-11
4p4.96-98
5p2.32-34
5m3.45-47

Idiomatic and
   Intellectually
   Complex Latin,
   Naturalizations
   of: 88-95,
   100-102
1p1.27
1p1.34-35
1p1.35
1p1.36-38
1p1.40
1p2.27-28
1m3.13
1p3.44
1m4.5-12
1p4.111-12
1p4.168-69
1p4.200-201
1p5.25-31
1p5.73
2p1.103
2m2.1-7
2p4.132-33
2p4.178-80
2p5.8-10
2p5.187-88
2p6.22
2p6.34-35
2p6.91-92
2p7.58-59
2p7.60
2p7.133-34

2m7.26-27
3p1.47-48
3p3.87-88
3p4.43-44
3p8.56-57
3m9.3-5
3p10.163-67
3m10.26-27
3p12.106-107
4m1.4
4p2.80
4p4.26-27
4p6.1-2
4p6.31-32
5p3.144-49
5p4.174-78
5p6.281-82

Glosses: 103-104
3p4.69-74
4p6.22-24
5m3.17-27
5m3.40-42

Combined
   Translation—
   Syntactic: 96-97
3p10.25-30
3m10.5-6
4m5.30-36

Double Translations:
   97-99
2p1.93-94
2p4.61-63
3m12.61-63
4p6.18-20
4m6.52-53
5p4.141-42
5p6.261-66

Miscellaneous Stylistic
   Techniques:
   105-10
1p3.65-67
1m3.6-7
1m3.12-13
1m4.8-9
1p4.55-56
1m5.28
2p1.16-18
2p2.50
2p3.36
2p4.116
2p5.159-61
2p7.56-58
2p7.123
3p2.74-77
3m2.1-2
3p3.17-18
3p11.43 (145 n)
5p1.71-73

Syntactic
   Experimentation:
   116-17
3p3.41-42
3p3.43
3p3.44-45
3p3.69
3p3.73-74

Alternate Translations:
   118-21
2p5.162-64
2p6.61-66
4p6.200-203
5m3.29-33
5p4.33-36
5p6.13-15

160

Index of Names and Terms

Ablative Absolutes: 64-68, 74, 82
Adjectives, Expansion of: 70-71
Alternate Translations: 117-21, 124, 126, 143n

Balance of Phrasing: 101, 108-109
Baum, Paull F.: 107
Blake, N.F.: 121, 137n, 145n
Boccaccio, Giovanni: 2, 86, 131
Boitani, Piero: 133n
Brewer, D.S.: 7, 12
Brinchele, John: 135n
Browne, Sir Thomas: 111, 123, 147n
Burnley, David: 138n
Bynon, Theodora: 18

Calques: 18-20, 54, 55, 112, 139n
Catford, J.C.: 133-34n, 139n, 144n
Caxton, William: 6, 35, 121, 122-23, 137n, 145n
Chambers, R.W.: 147n
Chaucer, Geoffrey
  ABC; 134n
  Adam Scriveyn: 147n
  Astrolabe: 3, 5, 6, 61, 113, 121, 130, 131, 140n

"Boethian Balades": 6, 124
Book of the Duchess: 2
Clerk's Tale: 6, 134n
De Contemptu Mundi: 6, 134n
Equatorie of the Planetis: 6, 134n
Former Age: 123, 146n
Fortune: 146n
Knight's Tale: 2, 6, 86, 124
Melibee: 2, 6, 113, 121
Parson's Tale: 2, 6, 113, 121, 130
"Retraction": 3
Romaunt of the Rose: 2, 6, 76, 131, 137n, 145n
Second Nun's Tale: 130, 134n
Troilus and Criseyde: 2, 6, 9, 15, 83, 86, 123, 124, 131, 135n, 147n
Wife of Bath's Tale: 6
Chesterton, G.K.: 130
Chute, Marchette: 7, 60-61
Cicero: 93, 134n
Cline, James M.: 9, 63, 64, 66, 108-109, 134n
Combined Translation
  Lexical: 32-34, 54, 57
  Syntactic: 96-97, 126

161

INDEX OF NAMES AND TERMS

Conjunctions, Addition of: 79-82, 126
Cowling, George: 8

Denomy, Alex: 138n
Deschamps, Eustache: 2, 122-23
Donner, Morton: 138, 140n
Double Translations: 97-99, 105, 107, 110, 112, 118, 126, 143n
Doublets: 35-46, 54, 57, 86, 95, 96, 97, 99, 112, 126, 137n

Eckhardt, Caroline: 6, 76, 145n, 146-47n
Edward III: 124
Eiríksmál: 62
Elliott, Ralph: 8, 56, 75, 77, 78, 113, 144-45n
Ellis, Roger: 3, 64, 83-84, 85, 86, 134n, 137n, 139n, 144n, 148n

Fehlauer, Friedrich: 135n, 138n
Fischer, Olga: 50, 138n, 139n
French, Robert: 7
Fristedt, Sven: 3, 83, 143n

Gardner, John: 9
Geissman, Erwin: 36, 46
Glosses: 52, 102-105, 107, 110, 112, 113, 143n
Godwin, William: 126
Grammatical Shibboleths: 62-63, 83, 87, 140n
Green, Richard: 3, 121, 124, 145-46n
Grose, M.W.: 112

Horace: 134n
Hudson, Anne: 134n

Huntsman, Jeffrey: 136n

Idiomatic and Intellectually Complex Latin, Naturalization of: 87-96, 99-102, 107, 126
Idioms: 20-23, 53-54, 87
Impersonal Verbs: 72-74, 116
Individual Words: 14-18

Jefferson, B.L.: 9, 12, 17, 36, 55, 63, 66, 74, 78-79, 92, 108, 146n

King Alfred's *Consolation*: 128, 131, 138n
Koch, John: 148n
Kottler, Barnet: 7, 135n
Krapp, George: 8, 9, 60

Lawler, Traugott: 3, 54, 135n, 148n
Lawton, D.A.: 134n
Lewis, C.S.: 125
Lexical Derivatives: 36, 38, 43-53, 55, 112, 126, 137n, 138n
Lexical Errors: 14, 23-26
Lexical Experimentation: 34-35, 55-57, 114-16, 117, 124, 126
Liddell, Mark: 7, 143n
Lipson, Carol: 3
Lounsbury, Thomas: 35
Love, Nicholas: 148n
Lowes, J.L.: 146n
Lydgate, John: 6, 122-23

Medieval Wordlists: 13, 15-21, 25, 31-32, 46, 50, 54, 126, 136n
Meier, Hans H.: 133n
Minnis, Alastair: 144n

INDEX OF NAMES AND TERMS

Mukařovský, Jan: 138n
Mustanoja, T.F.: 141n

Neologisms: 27, 50-53, 55, 56-57, 114-16, 138n, 139n
Nonce Words: 56-57, 114-16, 140n

Oizumi, Akio: 138n
Open Translation: 3, 63-74, 79, 83, 140n

Pace, George B.: 135n
Parataxis: 65, 78-79, 142n
Participles: 68-72, 74, 79, 86, 141n
Payne, F. Anne: 131
Periphrasis: 26-32, 53, 54
Periphrastic Derivatives: 47-49, 57, 126
Peterson, Kate: 143n
Petrarch: 135n
Philip IV: 123
Preface, Absence of: 121-22, 124, 146n
Pseudo-Aquinas: 98, 143n
Purvey Preface: 4, 62, 63, 64, 65, 68, 134n, 143n

Remigius of Auxerre, Glosses of: 7, 103, 104, 110, 129, 144n
Richard II: 124
Robinson, F.N.: 8, 17, 60-61, 98, 112
Rolle, Richard: 54, 84, 139n
Root, R.K.: 8, 107
Roscow, Gregory: 142n
Ruggiers, Paul: 133n

Saintsbury, George: 8
Samuels, M.L.: 146n
Scheps, Walter: 140n
Schlauch, Margaret: 108, 144n
Schless, Howard: 133n
Sedgwick, Henry: 135n
Semantic Extension: 55
Shirley, John: 6, 122-23, 135n
Shoaf, R.A.: 133n
Silk, E.T.: 103, 135n
Skeat, W.W.: 107, 135n, 144n
Sources of Boece: 7, 103-104, 110, 111-12, 127-31
Spurgeon, Caroline: 7
Steiner, George: 133n
Stewart, H.F.: 7, 55, 107
St. Jerome: 4, 12, 63
St. John: 12
Syntactic Derivatives: 74-78, 82, 87, 112, 126, 140n
Syntactic Experimentation: 116-17, 124, 126

Thompson, W. Meredith: 133n
Tolkien, J.R.R.: 1, 10, 127
Translation: 2-5, 8-10, 112, 126
Trevet, Nicholas: 7, 98, 103-105, 110, 122, 129, 143-44n
Trevisa, Nicholas: 3, 4, 9, 54, 63, 64, 83, 84, 113, 141n, 143n

Usk, Thomas: 6

Voigts, Linda: 135n

Walton, John: 129, 146n
William of Aragon: 122, 146n
Windeatt, Barry: 133n
Workman, Samuel: 4, 83, 134n
Wycliffites: 3, 4, 9, 63, 64, 83, 84, 113, 141n, 143n